Woodworking Projects

Ultimate Guide To Woodworking Tools, Workshop Tips, Safety Precautions And Lots More

(Step-by-step Guide With Indoor And Outdoor Plans)

Clayton Kelvin

Published By **Chris David**

Clayton Kelvin

All Rights Reserved

Woodworking Projects: Ultimate Guide to Woodworking Tools, Workshop Tips, Safety Precautions and Lots More (Step-by-step Guide With Indoor and Outdoor Plans)

ISBN 978-1-77485-911-7

No part of this guidebook shall be reproduced in any form without permission in writing from the publisher except in the case of brief quotations embodied in critical articles or reviews.

Legal & Disclaimer

The information contained in this ebook is not designed to replace or take the place of any form of medicine or professional medical advice. The information in this ebook has been provided for educational & entertainment purposes only.

The information contained in this book has been compiled from sources deemed reliable, and it is accurate to the best of the Author's knowledge; however, the Author cannot guarantee its accuracy and validity and cannot be held liable for any errors or omissions. Changes are periodically made to this book. You must consult your doctor or get professional medical advice before using any of the suggested remedies, techniques, or information in this book.

Upon using the information contained in this book, you agree to hold harmless the Author from and against any damages, costs, and expenses, including any legal fees potentially resulting from the application of any of the information provided by this guide. This disclaimer applies to any damages or injury caused by the use and application, whether directly or indirectly, of any advice or information presented, whether for breach of contract, tort, negligence, personal injury, criminal intent, or under any other cause of action.

You agree to accept all risks of using the information presented inside this book. You need to consult a professional medical practitioner in order to ensure you are both able and healthy enough to participate in this program.

Table Of Contents

Chapter 1: Woodworking Tools That You Need 1

Chapter 2: The Basic Tools And Skills Of Woodworking 6

Chapter 3: How You Build A Trestle Table 18

Chapter 4: Wood Working For Newbies: Joinery Techniques 25

Chapter 5: Shaping Tips And Guides 38

Chapter 6: Which Projects Will Sell Most? 49

Chapter 7: Minimal Palletbed 54

Chapter 8: Projects For Living A Room Or Hall 61

Chapter 9: Tools Selection 79

Chapter 10: Must Have Tools For Woodworking 99

Chapter 11: Convenience Tools And Accessories 115

Chapter 12: Picking Wood 133

Chapter 13: Woodworking Tools 145

Chapter 14: Crosscutting Jig 157

Chapter 15: Woodworking Plans-What To Expect In Woodworking Plans 168

Chapter 16: Preparing A Surface 179

Conclusion 184

Chapter 1: Woodworking Tools That You Need

A woodworking toolman needs good tools! This chapter will help you to find the best tools for your woodworking needs. This chapter contains all of the essential woodworking tools that you'll ever need to be the best carpenter.

The Standard Hand Drill

The classic hand drill is a must-have tool for carpenters. This drill will enable you to tunnel through your wood materials on a fixed point. It is imperative that you have a hand-drill for woodworking. I haven't had any issues using the standard drill for my own hand drill.

The older cordless cordless drills may be more convenient than the standard hand drills. They are notoriously expensive and can be difficult to recharge. If you are just starting and require extra time for your work. I'm not trying to sell a product. However, the standard (cord-based), hand drill is one I recommend. The best thing for you is to have one of the above tools as soon as possible.

Tape Measurer

Without a good tape measure, it is unlikely that you will get much done. Even if you manage to put it together, it will likely be so crappy that it won't even be worth the time and effort you spent building it. You can purchase a high-quality tape measure at most hardware or home improvement stores.

One of the best things about this tape measuring device is its clearly-labeled "tics". These tics are small markings along the fiberglass (or metal) tape that will show you how to measure any surface. Tape measurers are your gatekeeper to accuracy. Use it!

These tape-measurers should work in either "imperial unit" or "metric". The tape measurer should be divided into inches and feet or centimeters & meters. These indications should appear for the entire length the tape measurer. Be sure to pay attention and keep an eye out for the indications!

Hand Saw

Every good carpenter knows that the hand saw is an important tool in their woodworking arsenal. It should not be left the toolbox without it. This is the traditional standard in wood cutting. Sharp teeth can be used to cut the toughest of stock wood materials. I have yet met a grain-based piece wood that a good saw could not cut quickly.

When it comes down to the art of woodworking, the common handsaw is your paintbrush. This is because it is the one you will use the most, and you can shape it from the beginning. This is your mode of operation for woodworking. This is your tool to make it all work together.

The common hand saw is cut in a cross-cut fashion, which makes it easy to glide across many wood surfaces. Yes, you should get one if your hand saw is not already purchased. Don't worry if it isn't possible to buy one. You can always borrow one. I'm sure your neighbor has one. No matter how you do this, just make sure to get one.

Power Jointer

This tool is more difficult and intimidating. However, you really don't need to be scared of the power jointer. This tool is used to make bends in your wood easier. You can think of it as an industrialized version or sandpaper. Sandpaper has been used for wood work for thousands upon thousands of years. This is the simplest way to smoothen out the rough edges.

Instead of spending 10 hours polishing your wood with a scrap of sandpaper, a power-joiner can make it easy to run it through the machine in just minutes. A power jointer is a tool that I use all the time. It really does work well into every wood detail. A good power jointer can help you create stunning woodwork with little effort.

Be sure to get a versatile jointer. The more traditional table top models have been known for limiting the work you can do. For the vast majority of woodworking projects, the "Rigid Power Jointer", is the best type of jointer that you can use.

Chapter 2: The Basic Tools And Skills Of Woodworking

If you are serious about woodworking, you should make it your top priority to purchase all the tools necessary. Most likely, most of the tools that you need are already available in your own house. You might still want to purchase additional pieces of equipment. To make sure you are always prepared for any unexpected situations, it might be worth replacing some of your tools. In any event, you need to know the basics of hand and power tools. Each category will be covered, along with the essential tools that each one should possess. We'll also examine some miscellaneous products that can be included in your shop tools chest.

Hand Tools

A selection of woodworking tools

Hand tools are the most cost-effective and easiest way to start woodwork. Here are some essential hand tools for a basic woodworking set.

Hammer

The clawhammer is one of the most easily recognized tools for woodworking. The clawed end allows you to drive nails into wood and also remove them. The clawed ends also serve as counterweights to balance the hammerhead. It can be useful for many other tasks.

The weight of the hammer is an important factor to consider when purchasing one. A heavier head means more power for each stroke of the hammer. This makes driving nails easier. This might make it a bit harder to control. When buying a hammer, another important consideration is the handle size. The longer the handle, you can swing the tool faster and increase the force. The preferred weight for a claw-hammer is approximately 450g.

Hand Saw

The handsaw is another tool used in woodworking. Even though power tools have been available, many skilled woodworkers still use hand saws.

Woodworkers feel it is essential that they have at the very least two different handsaws in a toolbox.

Ripsaw

Crosscut saw

There are many hand saws. The two most essential types to include in a starter kit, however, are the rip and crosscut. The main difference between the two saws lies in how they cut the wood. While the ripsaw cuts along a grain, the crosscut cuts across that grain. It is important to note that the number or teeth per inch (TPI) will determine which saw should be used to cut a particular wood stock. Higher TPI saws are better for smaller stock sizes, while lower TPI saws can be used for more severe cuts on larger stock.

If you don't need to handle two tools at once, you can purchase a saw with interchangeable knives.

Tape Measure

A retractable tape measure

For wood projects, accuracy is key. You want every piece to fit exactly to the dimensions. A tape measure is more convenient than a ruler for this purpose. It is compact and can be carried around easily. It is best to have a 25-foot retractable tap measure. Anything more than that will cause the retract mechanism not working correctly.

The strength of the hook at your tape measure is an important aspect to consider when purchasing it. It can become loose and cause measurements to be off by an eighth of an inch. Also,

Keep the tape from rolling back too hard to prevent damage to the tab.

Screwdriver

Set of interchangeable bits in a screwdriver. These bits are common sizes that can be used by all types of screwdrivers.

If you are looking to quickly disassemble joint pieces, screwdrivers will come in handy. But they can be a hassle if you don't have the right size of screwdriver. A good set should contain the most common sizes of flat-head and Philips screwdrivers.

It is not as common but it would be beneficial to have Torx drivers and Star drivers.

Chisel

A collection of woodworking and chisels

The chisel, which is commonly associated with woodcarving, is perhaps one of most overlooked basic tools. However, the versatile chisel can be useful for cleaning out saw cuts and joints. The chisel can also be used to pry apart two parts that have been joined.

It's a smart idea to buy several sizes of chisels when you are buying them. You will have a longer life expectancy if you choose chisels that are made from high carbon alloy steel or chromium/vanadium steel. These can withstand hammer hits well, so make sure to get hardwood grips with metal caps.

Hand Plane

Block Plane

Even though the handplane is often overlooked by beginners, it's an essential tool for any woodworking starter kit. This plane is used not only to smooth wood but also to shape and trim it to your desired dimensions. A block plane is an excellent tool to start with for novices. It's a great idea to buy older block planes as the quality of steel used in the parts is often much higher.

Power Tools

These power tools make it easier to complete common woodworking tasks faster and more efficiently. There are two kinds of these tools. One is corded which means you have to plug it into a wall outlet and the other is cordless which has its own battery pack. A majority of power tools come with several attachments. This allows them to do the work of multiple tools.

Circular Saw

Although the circular see is often considered to be more of an instrument for carpentry work, it has become essential for woodworkers. The circular saw is able to do saw-like cuts. It can also be adjusted to make precise cuts by using clamps. This is great for working with plywood or fiberboard.

Similar to the handsaw, the number and type of teeth that you use when making a circular or saw blade are important. A blade with more teeth makes it easier to make precise slices.

Jigsaw

It can be difficult to cut curves into pieces of wood with regular saws.

A jigsaw can make your work much easier because you have more control to direct the cut. Orbital action would be a great feature to have in a new jigsaw. Orbital action is a jigsaw that angles the blade forward. This allows for smoother cutting, as opposed to standard jigsaws where the blade moves up and down. You will find this feature in more expensive units.

Table Saw

Many beginners will find the table saw their first major purchase. This is because it is where most of the work will take place. A table saw allows you to both cut large chunks of wood and accurately trim smaller ones. Many table saws include components that can be used to let

You can choose from different thicknesses of lumber and cut them at the angles you prefer.

Drill for Power

This is another task that you'll encounter. It will surprise you to learn that a power drill corded will work better than one cordless. The reason is that corded power drills tend to be less expensive and provide constant power for longer periods.

Router

The router is a useful tool for beginners that can be used to accomplish a wide range of tasks. A

The stationary model is the best option for beginners because it can perform most tasks quickly. You should choose a unit that has at least 2HP, and is powerful enough to handle larger bits.

Random Orbital Sander

Random Orbital Sander w/ Sanding Disks

Sanding is probably the most tedious of all woodworking tasks. This is because you will need to spend many hours polishing the wood. The random orbital-sander makes it easier and takes away the hassle of rubbing the sandpaper onto the wood. Another advantage of the random orbital sander, is that it reduces visible sanding marks. It moves in an unpredictable motion and not following a defined pattern.

Miscellaneous Tools & Items

There are other tools that you need to have in your shop's inventory. These items are useful for a variety tasks and can also come in handy when you need improvised instruments.

Clamps

Clamps can be considered one of the most important tools you have in your shop. You can use them to hold glued pieces together until the glue sets. They also serve as a holding device for cutting pieces or clamping wood beams being bent into shape. There are many types available in clamps: corner clamps with C clamps, bar clamps for spring clamps or face clamps.

Pliers

While pliers are most commonly used for electronic and electrical work, they can also be used around the shop. As with clamps, pliers can also be used for holding pieces of wood during work. Pliers can also serve as a temporary wrench to loosen bolts from wooden panels or as a lever to pry pieces of wood.

Niveaux

It is essential that objects such as cabinets or tables be level when they are made. You can check this by using a level. The basic level consists of a small clear cylinder with liquid inside and a bubble suspended in it.

Speed Square & Builder's Square

A speed square can be used by a woodworker to check that pieces are aligned properly. The speedsquare is basically an L-shaped ruler.

Marking Tools

The carpenter pencil and chalk are two of the most useful tools for marking in the workshop. The chalk is the everyday type that you can buy at school supplies shops.

Work Is Important

Particularly useful for those who must deal with tight spaces, work stands are a great option. These are great for holding your tools so they aren't lying around. A work stand can also come in handy when you have to transfer between rooms.

Air Compressor

The majority of power tools you already own are electrically powered. But, some power tools, such as nail guns, can be powered with compressed air. The versatility of air compressors is not limited to powering pneumatic tools. They can also be used for running other equipment.

Chapter 3: How You Build A Trestle Table

Trestle tables are simple to make and allow for multiple design options. The top can be customized in numerous ways, including the stretcher between the trestles and the top. The design is simple and easy to use by diners. You can easily scale it up from a kitchen-sized table to a large dinner table. This trestle table has a key feature: the wedged joinery to support the stretcher. Although it's called knockdown the joinery is rock-solid. With a through-mortise-and-tenon joint, the stretcher locates and holds the trestles upright. It is an amazing feat of engineering that the wedges hold each item together, preventing the table from moving along its length. There is no stronger joint that I know of. It's also beautiful: The wedges and ventureing tenons add an extra design element. This section will be about stretcher joining, which is the most challenging aspect. It is important to fit the through-tenons correctly and the wedges properly to their respective mortises in order for the joinery to be successful.

How to cut mortises

* Furniture construction is like painting a flooring.

* Cautionary planning will keep you from falling behind the curves.

* To ensure a parallel reference for the router, it is essential to first cut and lay out the large through mortises in the posts.

* I create a template for a guide bushing, and a simple shopmade mortising device jig to rout mortises.

* The jig comprises a 1/4-inch MDF routing tool attached to a fence that registers with the stock.

* The jig centers your mortises on how wide the posts are, but you'll still need a layout.

* Measure the height of each post from the top to mark the tops & bottoms of the mortises.

*Utalize a square, to carry the lines around the board's other face. After that, confirm that the edges of both boards are parallel to ensure that the marks match up.

* Now, since the jig's slot is somewhat larger than that of the mortise, you will need to create a separate registration marking in order to pinpoint the jig.

* Fix the mortising templates securely on the outside of your post.

* To cut the mortises I use a plunger with a 3/8 inch spiral-fluted bit.

* You can either rout to the full depth of the post or stop there and remove the waste with a chisel.

* To make it work for posts with greater thickness, route away in shallow passes at half the mortise depth.

* Remove the template from the workpiece and flip it over.

* Next, remove the mortises from their holes and cut them out square.

* Now, you can make those posts.

How to trim tenons

* Because the stretcher is large, it can be difficult to handle.

* In one example, it is too long for a tablesaw tensioning jig to safely support.

* It doesn't really matter what tenoning techniques you use. Your tenon's fit is visible at the point where it exits from the big throughmortise.

* Joinery comes before shaping, as with the large posts.

* After I had laid out the stretcher shapes and tenon locations, I cut the shoulders with the tablesaw.

* To trim the tenon cheeks, I set up a roller support on the bandsaw. Also, I attach a 6-tpi blade to the outside of the bandsaw for smoothness.

* Before cutting the Tenon to width, I make sure to clean up any cheek cuts and trim the Tenon to the right thickness.

* I use a shoulderplan to keep the cheeks in line with the shoulder. I can also switch to a blocking plane for stock removal closer the tenon ends.

* The last 2 inches or so of the Tenon will not be housed within the assembled joint.

* I also cut out the tenon at the same time on the bandsaw. Once again, leaving it slightly oversized and cleaning up with my hand equipment until it slips through the mortise without any gaps.

How to wedge mortises

* The mortise is the last step of making the tenon.

* Cut the mortise across the entire width of your tenon. However, it is important to cut the outer mortise at a 8 degree angle.

* The secret is that you can simply cut the entire mortise at 8 degrees using the drill press.

* If your drill presse doesn't have tilting tables, you can use a jig.

* Mark the wedge hole with a line in the thickness of the tenon.

* Mark the mortise's end at 3/4" beyond the post. But, have it start 3/8" inside the post.

* This ensures that the wedge does not touch the mortise at the back.

* Before you use a bradpoint bit, first drill the holes at the mortise's ends.

* Don't rush and take your time.

* Next, drill the middle.

* To remove the rest of the waste, clamp a stretcher on the bench.

* Place the mortise in the middle, taking the workpiece from the top as well as the bottom. Flip the piece if necessary.

* Chamfer the wedge mortise to both the top & bottom, so the wedge slides more easily.

* I cut the wedges with the bandsaw.

* Position a sliding bevel at the angle to the mortise. Then, mark the shape with 1/4-inch MDF.

* Cut out the shape you want and then file the edges.

* Attach another piece MDF (or glue) to the bottom part of the template to secure the workpiece.

* Create wedge stock of the right thickness and length.

* Now, cut the wedge using the bandsaw fence.

* Hold the wedges in a vise or a jig on the shooting board while you clean them.

Chapter 4: Wood Working For Newbies: Joinery Techniques

Woodworking is the art of joining two pieces to make furniture, boxes, and other objects with edges. Joinery can be described as a core concept in woodworking. There are many kinds of joints. Some of these we'll talk about in this chapter.

Before you decide which type of wood joint you want to use for your project, it is important that the joint's inherent strength and weaknesses are known. It is important that the joints you choose are strong enough to withstand the pressure that your piece will experience. Some joints will require fasteners and adhesives while others only rely upon the wood. Other joints will need nails or screws for stability. The following are some of the wood joint properties that you should consider when selecting a joint to be used on your project.

Combine strength and flexibility with an esthetic sense.

Some wood pieces can only be fastened using a butt joint, while others can also be used to attach decoratively (dovetails). You can combine two or more types of joint to increase strength and visual appeal.

Some joints can be very easy to make, while others are more difficult. Here are some basic wooden joints and how they can be properly executed.

Butt Joints

Butt joints join wood pieces at corners or edge-to–edge. Butt joints don't look good or are strong. A butt joint is usually cut at an angle (MITRE Joint) to enhance aesthetics. You can strengthen your joints using glue, blocks, screws, or both. You want a quality butt-joint, so ensure that the stock ends are as straight as possible.

How to Make Butt Joints

Step 1: Measure the length and width of your timber with a tape measure. Use a pencil and a trysquare to mark straight lines where your timber will be cut.

Step 2 - Next, use a mitersaw to cut the lumber along your line. For your next piece of wood, repeat steps 1 and 2. Drill the holes carefully if you are going to use dowel drills for the joint.

Step 3 - Secure the first timber piece on your bench by using clamps and vices. Keep the timber flush to the bench top.

Step 4 Apply a little glue on top of the lumber. Now, align the edges of the timber pieces directly on top. Grab the pieces by securing them together.

Step 5 - Next, use glue and make sure your joint is square before you start nailing.

Tip: Insert a square or rectangular piece of wood into your butt joints to strengthen them or stop movement.

Miter Joints

The Miter joint can be made by making a corner or sawing each end to 45 degrees. It is more appealing than abutt joint and is stronger. Drop saws provide the best miter joint results.

How to Make Miter Joints

Step 1 - Draw 45deg lines along both timber pieces - at the point where you'll attach the MITER joint.

Step 2: Make the cuts using a dropsaw, handsaw, or a circular saw.

Step 3 - Check the accuracy of your joint, then glue the two pieces together. Let it dry.

Biscuit Joints

With a biscuit joiner, biscuit-shaped pieces are used to insert timber pieces into holes that have been cut out of biscuits. It's decorative, but not very common, and is used mainly for joining large wooden boards such a table top.

How to make biscuit joints

Step 1 - Align two pieces on the bench with a pencil and draw some lines to mark the place where you will put the joint.

Step 2 - Secure the wood on a table or in a vice. The biscuit size will determine how the biscuit joiner is adjusted. Make a cut in the wood.

Step 3: Examine if the boards connect flush and neatly. The boards should be clamped together with adhesive.

Tip: Sand any timber joints that are uneven.

Dove Tail Joints

Dovetail joints can be strong and durable. They are resistant to being pulled apart. You can use it to join the sides and front of a drawer. A series pins that extend from one end of a board are placed into tails which are cut into an other board's edge. Tails and pins are trapezoidal in shape. The joint can be glued once it is cured.

How to make dove tail joints

Step 1 - Mark a line at the one end of the first piece of timber. Make sure it is as wide and deep as your second piece. Make sure you mark the line on all sides, faces and ends of the timber.

Step 2 - Now mark the dovetails. You have many options, but the best tool is a dovetail indicator.

Step 3 - Use a sharp knife to make straight cuts along each line. To avoid scratching the remaining pins you should only cut the timber. Mark an "X" on the pins to be removed.

Step 4 - Cut your dovetails on a bandsaw/dovetail saw. If you're using the band saw, make sure you follow your lines and don't stray too far from the marks.

Step 5 - Clean up the joints with a Stanley blade or chisel.

Step 6 - Prepare the second piece from wood by using the template of the first. You can secure the second piece onto the bench by using a vice. Then, place your first piece in alignment with your second.

Step 7 - Mark the lines on the timbers' faces as long the timber is thick. These lines create pins that will connect with the dovetail. Be very precise.

Step 8 - Cut the pins using the same procedure as step 4. Make sure to clean all cuts. You should ensure that your joints are flush.

Step 9 - Join the pieces together using glue. You can use the dovetail clips to secure the joints while they dry.

Tip: Make sure to use larger dovetails, pins, or other means of covering the joints when making drawers.

Dado Joints

A dado refers to a rectangular cut in a wooden plank that allows another piece to fit tightly into it. A dado join is formed when a dado from one piece is received with a similarly-cut edge of another. The dado can be viewed in cross-section. The pieces are then attached using glue, fasteners, and binding. Dado joints can also be found on wooden puzzle toys and bookcase shelves. You can cut the slots with a router using a jig and/or a saw.

How to make Dado Joints

Step 1: On your first wooden plank, draw two lines perpendicularly. Make sure they form a 90deg angle. Use a combination square. This is how you mark the dado's width and position.

Step 2: Continue to extend the combination square blades at least halfway up the plank. If the depth of your plank is 3/4 inch, for example, you would place the square 3/8 in deep. To mark the dado's beginning, place the square's knife against the corner of the plank.

Place the blade of the square against the corner to mark the dado's end.

Step 3: Use a miter or backsaw to make four incisions. Be sure to stop cutting kerfs towards the end. Use a chisel or a saw to remove any wood that is left between the cuts. You should check that the depth of the cuts is uniform.

Step 4 - Smoothen the bottom joint of the dado using a flat wooden filer. Clean the slot with a filer. Check that the other piece has the same design and thickness as your first piece.

Step 5 - Join the pieces and attach them together. Check that the pieces fit together. Put glue on the screws or nails to secure them.

Dowel Joints

Dowels are inserted on one wood piece and then placed in the holes for another piece. Finally, they are glued together. Dowel joints look great and are very strong. They can also be used to strengthen weaker joints such the butt joint. You will need a drill, as well as a dowel-centre (used to mark the locations of the holes).

How to make Dowel Joints

Step1: Find the right size dowel, then mark the joint. Make a hole in the first piece of wood. Then, mark the second piece with a dowel tool jig.

Step 2 - Drill the holes. Be sure to go as far and as deep as you can; your drill bit should not be smaller than your dowel.

Step 3 - Insert a dowel through one piece. Then, place the hole into the other piece and attach the dowel to the end. Glue your joint. If you are working with large pieces of timber, clamp.

Tip: A longer dowel is recommended if drilling a hole through a piece of wood. Remember that the dowel is visible from the back.

Mortise and Tenon Joints

M&T joints are strong and appealing due to their flush fitting design. This joint has an end which is secured into a slot similar to table legs. The projection of one piece is a Tenon. The slot on the other is a Morise.

The weight of the item determines the length and width of the tenons. There are several options for this joint: double tenons; haunched Mortises; tenons; and twin tenons. Twin and double tenons can be made by attaching two tenons to each other. While the tenons of the double are distinct, those of the twin are connected in the middle. To prevent twisting, the haunched variation is an extra half-inch of wood at the timber's end.

How to Make Mortise And Tenon (M&T), Joints

Step 1 - Mark out the mortise & tenons - tenons are first. Draw a line along the piece of wood, approximately 2/3rds of the depth of what you want to insert. Mark your tenon width. It should be approximately 1/3 of the timber thickness. Verify that your tenons correspond with your mortising drill bits or chisel sizes. If they don't, adjust the lines.

Step 2: With the timber piece in place, hold it at 45 degrees. Use a band saw to cut the tenon starting at the shoulders. You should follow the lines. After you reach the depth of tenon, flip the piece over and continue cutting.

Step 3 - Determine the position and then mark the mortise. Mark the mortise width using a tenon as a guide. Next, place the tenon across another timber and draw lines at the tenon edges. For the mortise to be deep, you will need to add two lines between the lines that have been drawn.

Step 4 - Now you can cut the mortise with a chisel, a mallet, or a mortising machine. It is much faster and easier to use a mortising device. To use the first method, first place the timber into a vice. Then, hammer the machine into the mortise. The machine is as simple as drilling into your mortise to remove the wood. Use a sharp tool to clean the slot.

Step 5 - Check that the entire tenon/mortise is properly aligned. If your tenon does NOT fit, use your band saw to cut more timber.

Step 6 - Perform a dry clamp test to ensure that everything fits. Once you're satisfied with the joint apply adhesive and clamp the pieces together. Be sure to get rid of any excess glue before you clamp to prevent glue stains.

The steps for the haunched version are the same as the regular, except that you leave extra wood in the mortise. Reduce the length of each tenon by half on one side. For the mortise, reduce it half as deep to allow for some room for the haunched section of the tenon.

Chapter 5: Shaping Tips And Guides

The first step to wood shaping is choosing a wood type. The wood type you choose may not be available if your wood piece is to be furniture. But if you can choose the wood that will be carved, then it is possible. Softwoods are easier to carve than hardwoods. This does not mean that woods borne out of coniferous trees are soft. Instead, it refers to more "obedient woods."

The wood's resistance to an indent is used to determine its softness. This scale is known as the Janca scale. However, an easy way to test wood's softness is to press down on the nail with your finger. Not angiosperms but hardwoods can be shaped, carved and painted. It's easier to use softer woods. You are a novice, so the softer the better.

Next is getting your tools. This should not be difficult since the previous paragraphs have dealt with shaping tools. Now let's get on to the carving.

A clamp is a good way to secure your wood piece to a smooth surface. This is essential because carving can become very tedious if the object is not controlled. The clamp serves as a grip in the early stages of carving. However, it is important to ensure that the clamp doesn't add pressure to the wood being carved. Otherwise, this can cause indentation. This can be visible in softer woods.

Below are details about the different tools you can use, such as the chisel or mallet, and the gauge. From the simplest tools to the most complex, move up. Once you have an idea or sketch of your piece, use a rough rasp.

You can use the curved rasp to straighten curvy portions of your piece. Use the straight portion of the rough rasp for straighter parts. You can also use diagonal motions with the straight part. After you've gotten a better-formed item, you can swap out the rough rasp to make a smoother one. This will create a better-formed piece. Finish the job with sandpaper of coarse grit. The definition of a smooth rasp is less than that of coarse sandpaper. Make sure to maintain a smooth motion and keep the piece round at all times. You can start with a rough rasp from the beginning, and go all the way to the end. Refrain from attempting to finish a piece first before moving on to the next. This will make it uneven. To achieve a more rewarding result, be patient. At this point, your product will have more detail and is fine-graded. You can finish it off with fine-grit sandpaper. You have your own carved piece.

Tips for laying and scribing

Scribing is a process that involves placing edges of wood on uneven surfaces to create a snug fit. Although it is difficult, this process can be done easily. These are just a few tips.

* You will need a compass and a jigsaw.

These three tools are all that you need.

* To get accurate readings, ensure that your compass pencil has a sharp point.

* A short pencil is better than one that is longer than the compass arms. This makes it easier for you to use the scribes. Your hand doesn't move the pencil, and the pencil doesn't confuse your eyes.

* Make sure you measure accurately the edge of each piece of wood.

* Next, position the wood on the surface. The metal arm of your compasses will help you trace the edge. As the metal end of your compass is lowered to the surface, the pencil would draw the bumps and roughness onto the wood. You can make sure that the space between compass arms are not too big or too small. If the space between the compass arms is not too wide or too small, you'll know it's right.

Once you have completed this, you can now go to your jigsaw and remove any wood that is not needed. It's a good idea to have a jigsaw, as there may be curves in your trace. If not, you can use any type of saw.

* Next, place the shaped wood form against the intended surface. Check to see if it fits. The file can be used to trim the wood if necessary. Here are some guidelines for scribing.

How to measure accuracy

Nothing is worse than trying to put together pieces only for them not to fit. It's better not to measure twice, than to cut one. However, sometimes double measurements can be disastrous. Here are some tips to ensure perfect measurements.

Compare all measuring tools. An imperfect rule or two could make it less accurate. It's easy to pick out the odd one and not use it.

* Do not ignore the loose ends of old tape measures. This will also cause inaccuracies.

* Never forget to keep a hook-rule handy. A hook is a perfect measurement for marking out points on a wooden surface.

* Select rules with machine-engraved grades over printed ones. It is easy to measure the exact spot with a pencil that slides into it.

* Make sure to keep your measurements in writing while comparing and transferring so that you don't forget them. Use a notepad and tape measure with notepads to do this.

* Don't make mistakes and convert measurements constantly. Use an architect rule.

* Keep track of any old measuring instruments as they could have worn out.

Safety guidelines for woodworkers

Woodworking can be dangerous and requires powerful machinery. You should not let your guard down in a wood shop as you are a woodworker. Here are some safety tips that will keep you safe when working in a woodshop.

* Avoid wearing loose-fitting jewellery or clothes that are too tight.

* Always wear all required safety gear. Dust masks are essential to protect your lungs and lungs from the harmful effects of wood dust. Protect your eyes from wood chips by wearing safety glasses while you work. Also, make sure to wear safety headphones whenever you are using loud-sounding equipment.

* Protect your clothes against dust with an apron

* Don't use gloves. Though they might be suggested, leaving your hands exposed allows you to grip better. Also, you can feel machines and the wood so your fingers are always in line. While it might seem odd to keep track, true woodworkers realize how essential this rule really is.

If you don't like the progress of a project, it is important to keep your mind in the right place. Take a break to get out of your head and clear your mind. This will help you avoid mistakes that could prove to be hazardous.

This will allow you to be more clear-headed and help you understand the work better.

* Do not work if you are high or under the influence of drugs. This is, for obvious reasons, just as dangerous as driving while drunk. You shouldn't carry a handsaw if you are impaired or high. Avoid drinking and working.

* Keep your woodwork workspace neat at all costs. All items should be kept in their proper places.

* Don't work if you aren't tired. Go to sleep instead. If you are tired, you might be unable to continue with an activity. This can cause you to either feel exhausted or in a hurry. Both can lead to serious health problems.

These precautions should be followed when working with woodworking equipment.

* When working with a tablesaw, make sure to use all safety equipment.

* Always use an ergonomic handgrip for a tablesaw.

* You should not touch a machine unless you have finished reading and understanding all the information from the manufacturing sector.

* Never use a tool unless you are familiar with its operation, and saws in particular.

* Always maintain a healthy balance and good mental awareness before you turn on a machine.

* Use saws and other tools that exude dust. Make sure your dust vacuum is on and close by.

* Never leave your children alone if there are other children nearby.

* Before you leave, lock the workshop doors

* Make sure to have your phone nearby in an emergency.

* Maintain your machines. They should be kept clean, waxed and checked on a regular basis.

* Unplug all tools when not in usage.

Woodworking workshops are famous for producing sawdust. Dust collection is crucial to ensure a healthy environment and safety. Wood dust has been identified as cancer-causing. This brings to mind both the massive amounts of wood dust that can be found in a workshop and the microscopic amount that gets into the lungs every hour. Do you see why it is so critical to install an exhaust fan now?

A dust collector with pleated filters is also a good choice. These are the ones that filter the air without leaving behind dangerous particles.

There are many options for wood dust vacuums. However, machines that can absorb the dust where it is made have the highest efficiency. It is clear that machines with venting systems are safer and more efficient. Also, when deciding on the type and brand of machine you want to purchase, keep in mind that a power tool like a tablesaw equipped with a dust extraction venting system is more efficient than a tablesaw without one.

Finally, we have reached the end of the first volume in this beginner's manual. The book covers every aspect of wood behavior. From their types and descriptions to how to drill. Everything you need to know to be a woodworker, including how to deal with your table saw, where to place it, what workspace locations to use, the characteristics of tools, skills and techniques, has been explained in a beginner-friendly way. You will find all the information you need in the second volume. There are many great projects that can be done indoors or outdoors. Simple projects are also available for children. I hope you would put everything you learned here into practice, including the safety precautions. With the talents, skills, or resources you have, do what you can. There are no limits.

Chapter 6: Which Projects Will Sell Most?

Once you have all the tools you need, you can make products that you want to sell. These are the most popular items because they are in demand all the time. The market is dominated by woodworkers, who tend to make the best products.

Picture Frames & BookCases

These are not uncommon in the woodworking sector. That means they sell well. But it also means that you need to make your product stand out from the rest. Create a bookcase by using a chair or a picture frame with a unique design. You want to make your product standout from the rest. However there will likely always be someone who has seen your design before and they will often go after designs that are successful. This is a common situation in the woodworking sector.

Boxes

Ironically, despite having cardboard, many people still use it for many different purposes. For example, boxes are used for transferring precious items. Although they were not as popular when cardboard was first invented, these crafty items are still very much in fashion.

Utensils

As the natural movement is growing in power, wooden utensils are gaining popularity. Because throwing away a wooden knife or spoon is more sustainable than using plastic, they have seen a resurgence. These utensils come in unique and valuable designs, which can be used to offer a green alternative to people who are less concerned about wasting their time than those who see it as an advantage. It is difficult to make all types of utensils, but it is possible to sell ladles as well as spoons and wooden knives.

Birdhouses

Most birdhouses found at local warehouses aren't very appealing because there is no way to mass produce such a wide range of houses. This makes it easier for woodworkers with a good understanding of this particular industry to find work. This niche is not easy to find and takes more time.

Chairs

You can't find a house without one. A chair is an essential component of woodworking. There is a lot to choose from online so make sure you have unique ones. You can create chairs that look just like elves, chairs that are specifically made for kids or chairs that display a fan-based trait.

Items for children

Although a large majority of the population wants to buy their children manufactured toys, there are many parents that prefer toys made with old-fashioned timber. Woodworking toys for children sell quickly. This could be because of sentiments or safety measures to stop children from swallowing toxic substances found in many toys. A baby crib sells faster than any other product. Many parents want something that is unique and will make their child feel safe. My son, when he had his first baby, actually had a wooden one. However, it was expensive and made by someone who was skilled in building cribs.

Desktops & Tables

There are many models that can be mass-produced, but some people prefer a custom desk or table. What person wouldn't love a desk that matches their style or complements their wall art? Individuals also desire tables that can be extended or broken into multiple pieces so they can customize their table to suit their occasion. Some of the most passionate players of Magic the Gathering even want their battlefields to be etched directly into the wood of their tables. Other than that, desktops and basic tables still sell very well, especially when they're a deep rich shade that is hard to find anywhere else.

Fan-Based Crafts

Magic the Gathering lovers and others can create items from wood that match their favorite genres, as we have mentioned. Cosplay is a huge industry that has a market value of billions of dollars. It also includes swords made out of wood, as it is impossible to craft a real sword out metal due to the design like Cloud's Sword from Final Fantasy 7. Twenty-two-sided dice sell for $5 to $20 each, depending on the design. A portable gaming station where you can store all the materials necessary to play a game of cards can be purchased for as low as tens or hundreds of dollars. Woodworkers are known to keep this aspect of their business open, as it can generate significant sales at certain times of each year, like the months leading into Comic-Con.

Chapter 7: Minimal Palletbed

Did you know that bed frames are becoming more rare? People prefer to buy box-type beds. These look great but aren't easy to move. Storage is also a problem. Many people prefer to have a regular frame for their bed so that they can store small items underneath, such as boxes or folding furniture. Don't waste that space!

This project will involve you sleeping with two people, so it is essential that it is strong. Start by picking up your pallets. It is important to ensure you only buy pallets made from sturdy wood that has no obvious weaknesses. Even if your bed is great, poor quality materials could make it unstable, creaky, or simply unable to support your weight.

What you will require

Depending upon the size of the pallets, you will need three to four. If possible, two pallets should be used for the main surface.

A saw (powersaws are better, but hand saws will work fine)

Wood screws

Power drill

Sand paper or power-sander

Paint or varnish (if desired)

Making This Project

Did you manage to find pallets that were the right size for your surface without having to be cut? That's a good thing, and it is also preferable. You will need to cut them down to the proper size.

You and your partner should measure the length of the bed and its width to ensure you are both comfortable. If you don't want to have very unstable pallets, leave the support beams made of wood holding the pallet planks firmly together.

Use the extra pallet or two that you have, and take some planks. This can be done by attaching them across the planks on the pallets so that they face up.

Now, you can have fun and sand your wood. This tedious task is best accomplished with a power sander.

Put the pallets together, and mark where your screws will be placed. To ensure that the pallets are even, you should place the soon to be tops of each pallet face down.

Drill holes in the areas where screws will go in.

You can either make blocks using pallet planks or extra pallets. These will serve as your legs. You'll need to drill holes where they'll be attached.

It's time to paint or varnish everything.

Assemble the parts using glue. You're done!

Food Serving Carts on Wheels

It is possible that you have enough furniture for your sitting area. Do you have a place to store things you do not use? These items could include snacks and drinks that have been served or will be soon. It's possible that you don't wish to add clutter to your coffee or dining room by buying unnecessary pieces. A portable little cart with wheels, such as a serving tray, can make life easier.

Even if the cart isn't used very often, it is great for keeping decorative objects. It requires very little materials and is easy to assemble.

What you'll require

A pallet can be small or large.

Hammer and nail

4 wheels for your bottom

Your choice: Pain or varnish

Sandpaper

Making This Project

If you don't know how to put this together, have a look at this image.

You will need to disassemble your pallet and take the pieces apart to make this cart. This makes it a great project for non-pallet wood (or if you don't have any).

Use two pieces of wood to build your top frame. Then join them with two smaller pieces. To get an even better idea, see the image.

Use pallet planks to create a surface above the top frame.

Continue the above steps for the bottom storage area.

To make the legs, cut four pieces of wood. Then attach everything together.

Attach your wheels to the bottom of your legs.

Sand everything, finish it, then paint it (if desired).

Pallet Plank Shelf

This is a simple and very useful type of shelf. You can make one in no more than a few minutes. You don't even have to use a complete pallet for this project. You can use any type of plank of lumber that you find. Palletwood is, obviously, one of the most cost-effective options for DIYers who have a budget.

These shelves are ideal for places where you don't have enough space to place a real shelving unit.

Making This Project

Measure the wall on which you want to place your shelf. Hold the planks against it and mark where you'll have to cut.

You should cut each plank to the appropriate length

You will attach the planks lengthwise in a 90° fashion using the drill and wood screws. Take a look at the final image to see how it looks.

To avoid splitting the timber, drill holes for your screw heads first.

Mark where your hooks will be placed. If you don't own hooks, any other similar shape can be used, such as cupboard knobs (see picture). These can be placed evenly or in any other way you prefer.

Now that your holes have been marked, drill some holes. Attach your hooks.

The hooks or screws you used to attach them might be visible on the back side of the shelf. The shelf cannot be hung up like this, so it's important to remove any excess metal from the back. Use sandpaper on the surface to smoothen it down so it doesn't scratch your walls.

The picture hangers can be attached to the back shelf. You can also use some strong wire, if you don't have them. The shelf should be allowed to fall.

Now hang your shelf just like you would with a large painting.

Chapter 8: Projects For Living A Room Or Hall

For a box made of 2 22.5"x 8"x 3/4" pieces wood, you need to line up the ends.

You can align the corners with the framingsquare. Then measure 2" and 6, at both ends, and mark on. Keep your board on for a while.

First drill holes along the trail. Then attach the four wood screws on each side. For interior shelves, add 22.5 x 8 x 3/4 inches of wood to the top frame. Then place the 16"x8", x 3/4" piece. Attach the wooden screws to the board.

Attach decorative panels onto your 36"x24", x 3/4' decorative panels on a wood piece (which will be desk doors). This will allow you to create your own design before you see them from below. Put the decorative panels on a piece of wood and paint them with your choice color.

Allow them to dry thoroughly before you paint the doors or desk frames.

Glue decorative panel for doors

It can be attached with wood glue sticks. Allow the glue time to dry thoroughly before moving your door.

Attach the hardware for the border or desk door

Flip the frame, so that the decorative panel are on the bottom. Then, line it up with the frame.

2 Connect the rock at the bottom of the door to the frame with cabinet hinges. Eight wooden screws are used to attach the hinges.

Then, use the sink hinges to connect the door and frame.

Line the hinge up with the rock bottom on right side of door and frame in--Mark the spot with a pencil to where you will need to drill holes with your wood screws.

First, drill each mark. Next, attach two wood screws. You can do the same thing for your left side.

Place the magnet hardware in place at the top right corner of your door. This is the second step.

Attach the magnet latch in the desk frame to align it with the magnet hardware.

Close the deck doors and mount the project on the wall.

This wall-mounted desk makes you feel like a fashionable piece of art when it's closed. When it's open, it feels small.

BOOKSHELF

A bookshelf is a solution if books are piled high on your desk, in front of your front door, or filled with plastic milk containers, Your bookshelf can be made in a few minutes. This guide will show you how to make a simple bookcase. But you can easily adjust the measurements to make a more functional case.

Design and measurements. You can build a bookcase for a specific spot in your house or make a unique shape to improve the spread of bookshelves.

Measure the area where the bookshelf is to be placed. The finished shelf unit should be approximately the same length and width as your measurements. Bookshelves have a traditional depth of 12 to 16 inches. But, you can customize the shelf unit to meet your needs.

Decide if your bookshelf's back will be open or closed. If you leave the back unlocked, your books will be able to rest or touch the wall behind your bookshelf.

Decide whether you'll use it for hardback, paperback, or coffee-table-size books. This shelter is adjustable to accommodate any size book.

You can choose from standard bookshelves that are two, three, or four shelves high. However, you can build as many cabinets as your project requires.

Choose the right wood. The final appearance of your piece and its cost and power will depend on the type of wood you select. As solid wood can often cost thousands of dollars, plywood with a hardwood laminate will be preferred. For the spine and shelves, use 3/4" plywood. The back can be made from 1/4" plywood.

A plywood sheet measures 4' in width, but a sawblade can fly 1/8. Calculate how many % 8 'longboards one sheet will yield and how many percent sheets will you need. One sheet is all you need for this project.

Choose the right scene. Cut your boards using a buzzsaw, a tablesaw or a saw. For the satisfaction of aligning your plywood, it is crucial to use a saw or a table saw.

Make your sides. Start by cutting your boards to the width you prefer. You should remember that the width standard is 12 " or 16". For this project, our depth will be 12 ". To achieve a cleaner cut ensure that you press the wood through all the saws at the same time.

Consider asking a friend or loved one to support you. Plywood comes in large, 4-by-8-inch sheets. This makes it difficult to manage on your own. You can support your plywood with sawhorses, or a roller-table.

A little "birch plywood", cut into a 12" wide strip. Make sure you use a straight through guide when using a buzzsaw.

. For two bookcase sides, you will need to cut the strip in 41 " pieces. This will allow you to adjust the length of your bookshelf by either reducing or increasing it.

Your bookshelf should be cut down so that it can fit on the shelves. Pay attention to the width of this saw. The blade width is 1/8".

Spreading 3/4" plywood on a piece of plywood 11 is a way to make shelves. 12 1/8" is required to make the bottom and highest shelves.

Take two strips and cut two lines. Next, make two more lines at the bottom.

You can trim the rabbet joints. A rabbit can dig little wood. The rabbi can make most of the bookcase by making his joints. The sides can then be squared, and you can securely pick.

Make a cut of 3/8 inches using a table saw. Make a straight line at the shelf's top using 1/8" increments, until the track is as wide as plywood.

Another option is to use ball-bearing, piloted to make your cut. Use a router that has a rabbeting bit.

You can drill holes for adjustable shelving to be installed along the bookshelf sides. Your shelves can be adjusted because of the differences in book size. It is best to arrange your books and have them rearranged in the most efficient way.

They were pressing a board (which will serve as your template for holes) in the following order: Primary holes are 4 "up" and 4 "under" the middle shelf.

You don't need a pegboard to drill holes. Instead, use the series of holes that are in the same spot from within to create a template for hole drilling using a pine trick. It should be the same length as Bucks' template board bore. You will need a drill/driver with a 4-inch bit to accomplish this. Use

A drilling bit of the exact same diameter. Because of shelf-support pins and drill holes in two "strings to 2" increments.

The depth of the pegs should be approximately 1/4 inch. Place a bit of tape on the drill stop to allow you to consider your guidance and the thickness of the pegboard before drilling to the desired depth.

Assembly

Maximum enclosed edges. Glue to Glue. To secure the highest, use pocket screws

Add folded support block. You can also use support blocks for the middle or lower shelves. Without adding bulk, reinforce the frame. These blocks should be attached to the frame.

Glue in place for the middle 1 "x 2 support blocks. Finish the shelf and attach them. Protect the

Nails. Run the nails until they are above the wood's surface. After that, use a pin and drive slightly below it.

Attach the pilot holes for drill and countersink attachments to the highest point of the bookshelf. Glue, 2 "wooden." Thank you.

Place the bottom and middle shelves on their respective positions. After you have secured the bookshelf to the highest position, attach the rock-bottom shelf.

Apply wood glue on the support block for the rock-bottom shelf, and place the stand.

Drill the edge of your bookshelf. Secure the shelf with 2 "wooden screws" (count link pilot hole)

If you are using the support block for the middle shelf, you can install it as soon as possible, just like you did on the rock-bottom shelf.

They are attached on the back panel. The back panel gives bookshelves a finished look.

Check that the bookshelf has a square shape. Adjust any screws to ensure the bookcase is at the right angle. To move the shelf.

She was measuring and cutting back the rear panel.

To secure the rear panel, lock it in place, you should start at one corner.

Attach trim. You can trim or mold your bookshelf according to your needs. I will take a look. A built-in unit can be created if the trim is sized to fit into a specific area of your home.

The sides and bottom edges of this book are 1" x 2 with sixpenny nails & glue. "Trim.

You may need to trim the corners.

Once the trim is installed, you can smoothen the sharp edges using a router with a 1/2" round on bit.

Don't cut the molding.

To hide the plywood edges, you can use veneer banding rather than molding to give it a sleeker look.

Iron the edge banding of birch plywood to the edges, shelves, and bottom using an iron set for heating the coffee.

Finally, press the veneer tightly. Plywood uses a J-roller. The outside can be cut lengthwise using a handy knife.

Use a veneer trimming tool to close the Carolinas' edges that are not directly touching the ground. After this, hand-sand the edges using a 120-grit Sandpaper until the edges are smooth. Plywood.

You can finish the bookshelf by sanding it. For the final appearance and success of the staining process, proper sanding will be essential. The staining will appear darker and more blurred if it is not properly sanded.

For best results, use. 150 grit is sandpaper with raised grains.

To cover the surface with 100% pressure, you can use a pad and sander or a handblock. Sand encompasses the whole body. Do not look for any sand that is irregular.

Seal or paint the unit. Protect your bookcase by coating it with a transparent or painted protective coating.

Apply primer and paint. The primer allows the stain to absorb evenly so that the wood is finished evenly. After priming, let it dry. Lightly shake the unit and then remove any dust using cheesecloth, a soft cotton towel or a cloth. Finally, paint the unit. After drying, apply sand, dust and the final coat.

You can choose white primer for a light-colored paint. For a deeper shade, you should choose gray. To match the color in your paint, your primer will also be tinted.

Use a transparent coating. Use a transparent, polyurethane coat if you choose exotic wood for your bookshelf. Allow the primary coat to dry, then use a fine-grit stone sandpaper to sand. You can remove the dust with cheesecloth or a soft cotton pad and then apply a second coat. Once again let it dry, before using a fine piece or sandpaper to sand it. Apply the third and last coat of finish.

Do not waste time applying twice. Put on a light, comfortable coat. Most small bubbles will begin on their own. If you don't deposit the sand, they will be fixed.

How to Make Temporary Cabinets

Step 1, Wall Walls Measurement

Find your spot and make a wood move mold at your local shop. Here, we made one cut2 of poplar to be cut into four wades. One more piece of 1/2 poplar was cut and then the remaining amount was cut into one x2x. We used comprehensive parts. The boards had a length that was custom-made for our location. They can be tilted according to your dimensions and sizes. We made two shelves so we had two sets.

Step 2 - Apply glue

Place a 4. Place a flat piece of large-sized wood on one side. Wood glue should be applied to the poles on your remaining two segments. Place them flattened against a 4-piece wide selection at the sides. This can form an "L". This can be made from wood. Let wood glue dry.

Step 3 - Nail

Add them to the sides of where you glued wood by putting them through the rock-bottom shelf.

Step 4 - Painting

The shelf can be painted white or any other color that you like. It will also require a couple of coats for comb strokes. Allow it to dry overnight.

Step 5 - To hang the shelf, attach the holes with a router. Or, you could pierce the shelf's end into a wall. You can flatten the frames using the A-level. Be sure to search the walls for the studs, and drill the screws through the bracket.

You will probably cover these holes with artwork, pictures, or books that are not intended to be kept on the shelf. If you don't want holes in your shelf, you have the option to route them into the back or add them yourself. Once you have drilled holes in the wall, attach the frame as follows: Your shelves can be staged to draw attention!

HEXAGON SHELVES

Step 1 - Cut each piece so that it measures 5.5. So that all pieces fit together, each board should be cut at 30 degree angles.

If you are looking to build bigger shelves, feel free to adjust the lengths of your pieces. Cut them at a 30-degree angle for a similar size.

All of your pieces are the same length. Keep the focus in place and you will be cutting in the opposite direction.

Step 2 - SAND

The board was very comfortable to use and easy to navigate. However, I wanted to visit another country so I didn't take too long to complete this step. My main goal was to eliminate the water from the area where I had cut the wood. Therefore, I quickly went over the sides with 80-grit Sandpaper.

Step 3 - ASSEMBLE

Once the sand has dried, turn six of your boards so that they face downward. Use 2-3 pieces each of blue painter's tap to tape your boards.

Frog Tape is our favorite, but it worked better when we were putting together wooden pieces.

Flip your boards in the same order as the tape.

Glue all edges of your boards. Be sure to stick to the glue, despite the sting. I like to draw a line of glue under the center and then spread it with my fingers. It can also prevent gum squeezing.

Turn your boards carefully so that they stand upright.

You can fold your edges into a hexagon. Check that all parts are secure and that tape is not damaged.

Step 4 - Tape.

The glue should be removed after it has dried. Ensure that glue is removed from any area.

If you are looking for extra assistance, you can place wider nails between the boards.

Step 5 - Paint or stain

You can stain or close your wood if glue dries.

If you'd like, you can seal them to your shelves following the instructions for your particular seal.

Notice: If you decide to stain your boards prior to gluing, they must be dehydrated first. The tape will not adhere properly to the boards.

Step 6 - Shelves

Hang To hang them, we first attached them using glue & nails. We connected the D rings to the plane at each end of the two shelves. Two shelves were divided by D-rings.

To hold your shelves, you can also use sawtooth hooks if you aren't removing more than one cabinet.

Chapter 9: Tools Selection

As with any other craft year after year woodworking continues its growth. The original tools were used for this purpose 500 years ago. They have been upgraded and improved upon or completely abandoned and thrown away.

There are many modern woodworking instruments available, but today we will be focusing on those you can and can use as a start point for your woodworking projects.

Not only are tools easier for woodworkers, but they also make your job more enjoyable. The best woodworkers are those who use the best tools. This chapter includes a discussion of the basics and a selection of tools.

WOODWORKING SHAWS

Circular saw

It is the only saw that can be used to power activate a beginner's saw. Although circular saws are available from different manufacturers, they have similar features. It has a wide blade with sharp teeth, which can cut through wood. All circular saws come with different capacities and are powered by an electrical current. Most are corded, and run on household power. However, cordless circular s saws are a great development.

The most popular saw among woodworkers is the circular saw. This saw can be used for anything from rough carpentry, to fine woodworking. Circular saws, however, can be misleading. They cut straight, smooth lines. It really depends on the type of blade you are using.

Three types include circular saw blades.

* Ripping Blades - Cut material lengthwise along or with the grain

* Crosscut Blades are used to cross-saw grain

* Combination Blades - Designed for cross-cutting and tormenting

The teeth pattern refers to the differences among the blades. Ripping blades have even spacing while crosscuts have wavy teeth. Combination knives have both styles. If you are tight on funds, it is better for you to get a good combination blade and carbide teeth. It's important to know the differences between blade diameters. The smallest circular saw blades measure 7 1/2" in diameter. But, 10" blades can be found, and larger woodcutting diameters up to 12" are possible.

Circular saws come in two different designs. The direct drive has the blade mounted directly to the motor, and the arbor at 90 degrees. Direct drives are most popular and cost-effective. Heavy work is best done with a worn circular drive. The blade patterns are unchanged, but the blade has been replaced by a piston-driven one.

JIGSAW

Due to its reciprocating tip that resembles a saber, the Jigsaw is a must-have tool for woodworkers. These machines use electricity to make intricate cuts. If you look at the lines of a jigsaw puzzle you will see how it can be used.

Jigsaws can be used in a variety of ways. Jigsaws have rotating blades that can cut in a reverse or up-and-down motion. Blades are different in terms of the number and shape. They can be used for cutting both metal and plastic. Fine-tooth knives are used for sawing veneers. On the other hand, coarse tooth-blades allow for quick and rough operation.

You can use one hand to operate this saw. This gives you the opportunity to use your opposite hand to hold your work. Jigsaws make small, intricate pieces with great precision. The best use for a jigsaw is interior cuts. After some practice, you'll be able make plunge cuts using your jigsaw.

COMPOUND MITERSAW

These saws are an upgrade to the standard circular but have the same crosscut/rip and combination blades as a conventional circular saw. They can be used in a track or arm, just like the radial arms saws they nearly replaced. While the most common blade diameters for crosscut saw blades is 10 inches and 12 inches respectively, the smaller 71/2" version can be used with compound-miter saws. It is important to use a high quality crosscut saw with a mitersaw.

Mitersaws are extremely versatile tools. They have replaced the backsaw and miter box in most shops. For compound angles and miters, such as bevels or miters (or any combination thereof), beginners will find that powered mitersaws can make more precise cuts. They can be fixed to regular angles (22 1/2, 45 and 90 degrees), but they can also adjust for any angle between. This includes cutting to the left or right.

Powerful miter saws evolved from the old cut-off or chopsaw. You can get them with sliding arms or in lengthened versions. Because their powerheads are often tilted, it is possible to combine miter and vel cuts. With a compound mitersaw, almost every angle can be cut.

TABLE SAW

Table saws have the ability to make cutting cuts that others can't. They have a similar design to circular saws but are upside down so the blade is visible below the table. Blade angles and depth can be adjusted easily for precision.

There are three basic types of a table-saw. The best choice for beginners is to use all three. This will depend on the size of the job and the place. Either a fixed-table saw that can be moved around in the shop, or one that can be folded away.

* Table saws for cabinets are heavy and designed to stay in place. Their engines have a blade driven by a belt pulley mechanism and are housed in a lower cabinet. These machines can be used for anything from

wood-ripping to cutting panels. Many beginners prefer to have a centerpiece for their workspace: a cabinet-table.

* Lighter-duty benchtop table saws. They are lightweight and compact so that they can be easily moved around. Direct drive is what makes benchtop saws so heavy. These saws are light and portable, but they can be quite loud.

* Contractor tablesaws are the smallest saws. Contractors use them when time and space is limited for simple, fast cutting. The table saws of contractors are inexpensive and can be used to practice new tasks.

Bandsaw

These saws excel at cutting intricate curved pieces or splitting rough stock. This combination of circular and Sabre saws is used to power tools. The teeth are mounted onto a flat steel band which rotates around the lower and upper pulleys. A flat table with tilting legs is attached behind the pulleys.

Bandsaws comes in different sizes. It depends on what size stock you plan to use and how difficult you want to cut it. There are two important characteristics to consider when choosing the right size bandsaw.

* The depth capacit is the bandsaw's blade exposure between the pulleys. Face opening, also known as depth capacity, is the width of the bandsaw blade between the pulleys. This ranges for large machines from 4" for small bandsaws to 12" for larger ones. This determines how dense the material's power.

* The throat depth is measured from where the teeth of your blade meet the back of your support frame. This indicates how large the stock may be. It is possible to make curved cuts without turning the bench.

* Bandsaw tooth for short cuts are available in coarse and fine styles. Fine teeth allow for faster, smoother cutting. The blade width of bandsaws is very important. Large blades will last longer for ripping. However, thin blades allow for easier curved cutting.

Handsaws

Handsaws will be found in most woodwork shops because they are easy to use and inexpensive to buy. Handsaws make it easy to do quick, precise work. Contrary to other saws there are no bulky, heavy-weight, awkward cables or batteries which can die.

Handsaws were popular for hundreds and thousands of years. The basic idea behind handsaws is a dented-steel blade with a wooden handle. This allows them to move back and forth to cut the work. There are more to handsaw use than most beginners realize. These are just a few of the many types you can use with a handsaw:

* Dovetail handsaws for joint work: The best use of these handsaws is for fine dovetail joint work

* Keyhole handsaws: Used to cut inside holes

For woodworkers starting out, it is a wise decision to purchase a high-quality handsaw. A blunt or cheap blade can cause frustrations with your handssaw. An electric saw can't cut wood as fast as a sharp blade with excellent teeth.

SUPPLIES FOR WOODWORKING: PLANING/FILING, AND SANTING

Because of the rough edges and surfaces left behind by cuts, you will need to have some filing, planning and sanding supplies in order to finish your work. These are the things woodworkers should look into when they start, regardless of how high quality or fine their saw blades.

Planes

Planes are tools that can be used for cutting, not sanding. All types use fixed blades to cut wood fibers. Blade size, depth and thickness are two of the most important factors in determining how much material can been extracted at once.

A variety of names for planes will be heard, some even humorous. Both jack planes and Rabbet planes shave lumber, but they have different applications. Also, you might hear words like spokeshaves or blocks. You may even hear them called in numbers. These are the hand planes we recommend for beginners.

Jack Plane. These tools extract a lot material from a pass. It is a tool for "jack-of-all-trades". It is compatible with both straight and curved edges, for smoothing/joining, respectively.

Block Planes - These planes are smaller but more powerful. They are perfect for close work with very smooth joints.

Jointing planes: They can also be called jack planes. Jointers typically have long frames.

Rabbet Planes, used across the edge grain of boards to create right angle grooves. These joints are also known as rabbets.

Scraper Plans: Used to smoothen wood surfaces by removing fine fibers. These planes are sometimes called cabinet-scrapers.

Spokeshaves - Planes for hand-crafted angled surfaces. They were initially made to support wagon wheel spokes. But both woodworkers are able to use them.

Orbital Sander

It's normal for an orbital sander to be the electric wood finishing tool you are purchasing. These fast-acting machines can do the job faster than hand sanding. From orbital sanders to inline tools such as the belt sanders, these machines are different. They use sandpaper pad that rotates in circular or orbital patterns.

Take an aspherical abrasive Sandpaper disk and spin it in a circular motion using standard orbital Sanders. Although they are quick to remove material, they leave swirl marks. The best buy is a random orbital grinder. They aren't circulated. Instead, they oscillate spontaneously, smoothing the wood's surface and removing any marks.

Hand Files

Hand files are the best way to shape or smoothen. Quality steel hand files will last a long while and are very affordable to buy. Do not attempt to sharpen your hand file if they have become dull. Here are the main options for hand-files:

1. Rasps have coarse teeth and are rough-edged. This tool can be used to cut large quantities of wood without the need for finer tools.

2. Half-round files combine a one-sided, curved face with a flat surface to allow both sides to seamlessly use straight and curved surfaces.

3. Mill files have the faces flat on one side. These file have both rough and fine teeth. They also have teeth at the edges, which are useful for tight spaces.

4. These cutters are similar to handfiles, but they are designed as electric drill bit. The rotary abrasive action will remove the

material. There are many rotary files that can be used for cutting.

Hand files are used to sharpen other woodworking knives and bits. Metal files typically have fine teeth, and are made out of high-quality metal. You will often get the full value of what you buy.

ASSEMBLY TOOLS FOR WOODWORKING

The process of chopping and smoothing the wood is part of total woodworking. Once all the components are correctly sized and smooth enough for assembly, they can be put together. The two key factors that will make woodwork work well are: Precision joints need to be exact. The correct tools will be needed to assemble and securely fasten them. For beginners, however, these are some basic tools:

HAMMER

There is no one specific hammer to be used for woodworking. While the claw tool of a carpenter might look very similar to an all-purpose pounding tool for woodwork, there are hundreds more. Woodworking hammers are typically asked to do two tasks. It is to pry or pound. They perform well depending on several factors.

* Includes head design including weight and face size. Some heads, like finishinghammers, can be smooth. Some have serrated faces to grip nails and fasteners, as can be seen in framinghammers.

* The claw style plays an important part in the selection. Finishing and framing hammers are distinguished by their long claws. Framers have straighter edges for splitting materials.

* It is crucial to consider the composition of the handle for comfort. A majority of woodworking novices prefer a hammer hand made of wood or composite. They provide less shock when they are used for hitting. Framers love handles made of steel. The steel handles are more susceptible to shock but contribute more weight as the driving force

behind them is stronger. Even, steel handles don't quickly split.

* It is important that the entire weight be taken into account. The hammer's mass is measured in ounces. Lightweight hammers weigh between 8 and 10 ounces. You can find intermediate hammers weighing 16 to 20 ounces and heavy-duty hammers weighing 24 to 32.

Although hammers can be made in many ways, the purpose and composition of hammers are different. Before you purchase hammers, be sure to understand what they can be used for. Below are the main hammers you can use for woodworking.

1. All-purpose finishinghammers are very affordable. They are extremely useful and should be your first purchase.

2. Framing hammers are not an easy task. However, they are not necessary for most woodworking tasks.

3. Tack hammers work in the same way as drivers using brads. They're designed for smaller jobs and usually have only two heads.

MALLET

You shouldn't confuse hammers and mallets. Both are striking tools but have their own uses. Hammers are generally steel-faced. Other hammers may be brass or rubber. Mallets are made from large wooden or leather head and can be adjusted to fit various head sizes.

The difference between mallets and hammers is their shock-producing surface effect and striking shock. Mallets, which transmit shock instead of transmitting it to the surface, are much softer than hammers and can withstand shock. They are perfect for wood joints, as they leave no trace of strike.

It is not recommended to use a steel hammer on chisels. Because of the slash/jab effect caused by chisels, steel hammers can create a rough finish. The chisels can be tapped with a mallet to help them slice the wood smoothly with consistent pressure.

POWER DRILL

A power drill is a great tool for beginning woodworkers. Only a few old-time craftsmen use a brace, bit or hand drill. These electric-driven drills are frequently used in the workshop for so many reasons. They can be used for more than drilling holes. There are many extensions that can be purchased to convert the electric drilling tool into other tools.

When purchasing your first power-drill, it is worth considering a corded model. The drills that operate on 110/120-volt currents are more powerful and last longer than those with cordless motors. It is easy to forget that cords can be frustrating, but a weak charger will make it impossible for them to fail.

The voltage rating will determine if you want to use cordless power drilling tools. Early models were 7.5-volt. However, they were quickly updated. An 18-volt cordless drill would be a smart choice for beginners. They are not as expensive as 14-volt drills, and have a lot more power.

It is common to measure power drills by their chuck sizes. Common medium size is 3/8' and 1/2 heavy-duty. Drills can be purchased in key versions or keyless, which makes it easier to adjust parts.

SCREW GUN

Screws are strong all-round timber fasteners. These fasteners are strong and durable, so they can be disassembled, made temporary joints, or replaced when necessary. You may not want to use regular hand screwdrivers but investing in an electric screw gun makes it easier and faster to drive screws. Screw guns are extremely useful for projects that require many screws.

Screw guns are an extension to the power drill family. Most of the screw guns available today are cordless making them extremely handy. The main distinction between a true screw gun and power drill is in the chuck's inside shape. Screw guns are designed for inserting bit shanks which are hexagonal, six-sided, or both. This reduces slippage.

Chapter 10: Must Have Tools For Woodworking

Woodwork has many meanings for different people. Many woodworkers create strong and useful parts to relieve tension, and also exercise their creative muscles. They are enthusiastic and know that sawdust has many benefits. Others are aspiring to be professionals. They have the ability to construct furniture. However, it doesn't matter if they're master craftsmen or amateurs; you still need the proper woodwork tools. This comprehensive guide contains information about these devices. Here are the most important woodworking tools.

Sawhorses*

Workbench*

Most woodworkers who are just starting out are overwhelmed by the sheer number of resources available. They are able to bring expensive equipment, worth thousands of dollars, into their business. But, the majority of tools for novice woodworkers are not expensive or difficult. Woodworking tools for beginners should start with the basics. This will give you a sense that simplicity is what makes great work.

There are five levels available in basic woodworking equipment. These tools can be used to cut, assemble, measure and carry wooden pieces. These tool classes provide all the tools a woodworker may need to create simple to complicated objects. Below is a guide that will help you choose the right tools for your basic toolbox.

SAWS USEN FOR WOODWORKING

Material cutting is a key component of almost every woodworking project. The best and most intriguing pieces start with rough lengths of wood. Wood stock must be ribbed, then cut to form. The solution is a saw, which comes in a variety of sizes and types. These are great for different cutting tasks. This is the information you will need to begin creating your saws' collection.

CIRCULAR SHAW

One power-activated saw should be found in every beginner's box: a circular saw. There are many brands out there, but each has a common feature: a circular or round blade that cuts through the wood. All circular saws have an electric motor. They come in different power ratings. Although most are corded and run on household power, there have been many advancements in cordless circularsaws.

Some people believe that circular saws can be used more effectively for rough carpentry than fine woodworking. However, this is false. The circular saws on the other side cut straight and clean lines. Much depends on what blade you use.

There are three types to choose from when it comes to circular saw blades.

Blades: Used to sift through grain

Combination Blades: For crosscutting and ribbing.

The difference between blades comes down to the nature of their teeth. Ribblades are designed with uniformly spaced teeth. Transverse blades, on the other hand, have staggered or staggered dentition. All types of tooth can be accommodated by the blades. If money is an issue, you should consider investing in a carbide-fitted blade. You must also know the diameter of the blade.

Two distinct circular saw models are available. The blade is designed to be mounted at 90

You can find the degrees on both the engine or on the harbour. The most common, and least expensive, circular saws are direct drives. These circular drives are not meant for heavy-duty work and can be damaged. They still use the same blade designs, however the blade is longer than the piston.

JIGSAW

From the very beginning, every woodworker should purchase a quality puzzle. Saben saws are sometimes referred to by their identical, sabrelike comb. These power tools are designed to create complex, smooth and curved cuts. Consider the lines in a puzzle to understand how complicated a puzzle can be.

Jigsaws are completely different from circular sees. Jigsaws are able to move backwards or upwards due to their spinning blades. Blades are different in terms of tooth shape and number. They can be used for cutting wood, metal and plastic. Fine dental blades for veneer cutting are used, while coarse blades for fast and difficult work are used.

Jigsaws are simple to operate with one hand. You should use the other hand to do your work. Jigsaws have the ability to cut complex pieces into tiny pieces. A puzzle's best use is the inner cut. It is easy to drill a pilothole, then insert the blade. With some practice, you'll soon be able make plunge cuts on your jigsaw.

COMPOUND MITERSAW

Compound mitersaws offer a different alternative to standard circular sees. They come with the same snap, cut and blades as regular circular saws. These blades are attached to radial arm and track saws, which they have almost replaced. Common blades measure 10 and 12 inches in diameter, while compound mitersaws can have a shorter size (7 1/2). It is best to use a standard cross section saw blade for miter saws.

These electric saws have a lot of flexibility. The traditional miter box or backsaw has been updated by most shops. The miter-saws provide precise cuts for compound angles and bevels. It is simple to set it at standard angles of 90, 45, 22 1/22, and 90 degrees. But it can be adjusted for any angle in between. It is required to make right and left cuts.

Powered mitersaws were inspired by the classic cut-off and chop saws. The sliding-armed version increases the cutting range. Their powerheads tilt towards each side to allow for combination of bevel and miter cuts. With a compound wither saw, you can remove almost any number of angles.

TABLE SAW

A table saw was a popular tool for woodworkers who started earlier in the game. You can achieve difficult cuts with table saws that aren't possible with other types. They are similar to circular saws but upside-down so that the blade from either the table or the work surface is exposed. To improve precision, the blade's depth and angle can easily be adjusted.

Three types of tablesaws are available. They are perfect for beginners. It all depends on the size of the job. A fixed table saw may be needed to work in a workshop, while a portable saw is used for removal. These are the choices at your table.

The heavy table saws in the cabinet are designed to hold their place. Their name is derived from the fact their motors are situated in a lower armchair with an adjustable blade controlled by a pulley belt and belt system. These are excellent for all sorts of work, such as wood-rubbing or panel cutting. Many newbies choose tables as their central piece of the laboratory.

The benchtop tablesaws are lighter in weight. They are small enough to easily transport and store. Most benchtop saws can be operated by direct drive. While they can be compacted, direct drive still makes them noisy.

Contractor table saws create the tightest prototypes. The contractor table saws are ideal for fast, efficient cutting in tight spaces. For beginners, contractor table saws can be a great way to learn about the work of contractors.

When making a tablesaw (also called a chop saw or chopbox), you should always use a high-quality blade, such as rip scroll blades or carbide tips blades.

Bandsaw

To make complicated curved cuts or tear material, there is no better tool than a bandsaw. This power supply is a mix of circular and sabre saws. It connects the teeth to an endless looped flat-steel strip that rotates about the top and the bottom pulleys. A flat table is located between the sleeves and tilts for angles.

Depending upon the size of the stock that you are cutting and the complexity of your cuts, there two important features to look for in band saws. Each of these factors will influence the size of the band saw size.

Depth ability is the amount of blade between the pulleys that is visible. The face gap is also known by the number of teeth between the pulleys. This can be as high as 12 for small machines or 4 for larger ones. This indicates the material capability.

The throat depth is the distance between the teeth on the blade and the back of support's frame. This will determine the size of your stock. The ability to cut angled pieces where work needs be done is made easier by a deep throat.

Both the coarse and fine teeth can be used to make quick cuts or a smoother, slower cut. Bandsaw blade width is very important. Big blades provide greater security when slicing. While thin blades allow for easier curved cutting, they are less secure.

Standard band saw tires are best for better performance.

Handsaws

Handsaws are a staple in every shop of woodworkers. Handsaws make precise, detailed cuts so quickly and easily. Handsaws can be used without bulky weights, tormented cords, or batteries that don't die. Handsaws don't cost much to set up and are easy to transport.

These have been around for centuries. These have a simple steel blade and a wooden handle. They can be used to move the job forward and backward. Handsaw use is much more complicated than many people think.

You might be interested in these handsaw designs:

Handsaws ripping - Cut with wood grain

Cross-cutting a handsaw with the cross-cutting feature: Incorporate wood grain

Combination handsaws: Both rips as well as crosscuts can be done with these handsaws

Backsaws - Use rectangular blades when miter cutting with bracedback.

Carcase Handsaws : Longer, heavier hands Handsaws Coping

Dovetail handsaws for joint work: Handsaws keyhole: Made for cutting inner holes

The best handsaws for beginners should be purchased. Poor quality blades can lead to frustrations. A sharp blade that has excellent teeth can work as fast as an electrical screw and is just as accurate to wood.

FILING SUPPLIES, PLANING AND SANDING SUPPLIES USETED IN WOODWORKING

Once the wood pieces have been cut, it is necessary to finish them. No matter how skilled your pieces are, they still require some sort of filing, planning, or sanding. These are the things great woodworkers consider as well:

Planes

Planes, which are usually used instead abrasive-sanding machines, are cutting machines. Planes come in a variety of sizes and use a fixed-blade blade to shave and smoothen wood fibers. The main factors are the size of the blade, its depth, and how much material is withdrawn at once.

We'll show you some unusual or funny plane names. Although both jack and rabbet aircrafts shave timber, they can differ in their abilities. You may also hear words like joints, spokeshaves or lines. They will be easier to remember if you use numbers. Woodworkers starting out can explore many different hand planes.

Jack Plane. This tool is capable of extracting a lot in a short time. This tool can be used for both smoothing and joining straight and curved edges.

Block planes - These are smaller planes that can be more powerful. These are excellent for tight jobs where precise joints are necessary.

Jointing planes: Similar jack planes with smooth edges. Jointers usually have long frames.

Rabbet Planes - Used to trim right corners along the edge a grained plat. These joints are known by rabbits.

Scraper planes - These aircraft are designed to remove fine fibres from wooden surfaces to make them super smooth. These aircraft are also called scraper cabinets.

Spokeshaves: handplanes for curved surfaces. They were originally used to make wheel spokes. However, they are now available for all woodworkers.

Orbital Sander

If you are going to buy one electric wood finishing device, it should be an orbital. These fast-acting devices take away all pressure and speed up hand sanding. Orbital Sanders are different than inline instruments, such as belt sanders. Sandpaper pads rotate in an orbital or circular pattern.

Standard orbital Sanders circle the circular abrasive and transform into a disk of sandpaper.

But if they remove material fast, they may leave swirl marks which are hard to remove. A random orbital sander is your next purchase.

oscillate,

mark-free.

Or, they can leave the wood surface slick and smooth by themselves.

Hand Files

A wooden or smooth file is usually the best. The best quality steel file ones will last longer than hand files and they are affordable. If your hand files become dull, sharpen them. Here are your top hand file choices:

Rasps refer to instruments with sharp teeth. They are used to remove large quantities wood for general shaping and then allow finer filers to take over.

Half-round file have a flat surface on one end and a curved lip on the other. This allows you work on both straight surfaces and curved ones.

The mill files on both ends are square. They are usually shaped with square corners. These have also close room teethed edges.

Rotary cutters look like paper, but with electric drill bits. These can be placed in your boiler chuck, and the material will be extracted using the rotary cutting action.

Available are rotary files in various patterns and grit cuts.

Metal files are usually made from high quality steel and have very fine teeth. Like any other device, you get what your pay for. However, investing in high quality hand files is worthwhile.

Chapter 11: Convenience Tools And Accessories

Woodworking can be difficult for those who aren't experienced. Simple projects can take a lot more time and effort than others. Sometimes it is easy to get overwhelmed by the sheer amount of work involved. But manufacturers have taken great care to design a variety of small ways to make woodworking simpler for their craftsmen.

Here's a list with useful woodworking tools on the current market:

The magnetic wrist nail holders are one example of a simple invention. The magnetic nail holder is made up of six magnets, which attach to the woodworker's wrist. This allows him to have up to one pound worth of drill bits, nail, etc. on his wrist for easy access. The woodworker can take his nail holder along with him on the road.

A miniature plane is a exact replica of the full-size plane, but it measures only a few inches long. They are smaller than regular planes. They can be used for precise smoothing of small wood surfaces, such the edge of a plywood sheet.

The Bowjack, a tool for installing wooden planks on ceilings and floors, is used for decking. The Bowjack can be placed alongside a board. Once the tool's spur has been inserted into wooden framing, the Bowjack will be activated. The Bowjack pulls the lever and the board is forced into its correct spacing and position. A sliding collar helps to keep the board in its place, so that a woodworker can use his hands to fasten the wooden boards onto the frame.

Steel straight edges last longer than wooden or plastic rulers. They can withstand any type of damage, including scoring. It is important to find a straight edge made from steel that has a precise level gauge.

Roll-up bags are lighter than standard tool boxes. Roll-up tool bags are made from thick polyester fabric. They can be used to organize, protect, and keep tools. A bag typically has enough pockets to hold nine tools and can be up to two inches wide. To stop tools falling out of pockets, a flap should be added. These bags can also be spread on a wall and made visible by the tools, which is slightly different from when in a toolbox.

Safety tethers are a unique safety device that prevents tools from striking woodworkers' feet or anyone else standing below. They are crucial for projects on "high ground", like roofing. Safety tethers made of stainless steel cord have a maximum strength to 175 kilograms and attaches to the woodworker's belt.

You are likely to find a product that will solve your woodworking problems. These products make it easier, safer, or just plain more convenient to do your project.

Plans and projects

Woodworking is both a profession and a hobby that can offer a lot fun and challenge. The thrill of seeing raw wood transformed into useful or beautiful products is part of the fun. It's also fun to plan how you will build something.

Woodworking projects are complex and require a lot of engineering, architecture, and math. Woodpieces can lose their structural integrity if they lack basic math skills. The majority of woodworkers are novices or not experienced enough to make these plans. Many skilled woodworkers prefer not to have to do the plans.

Premade woodworking blueprints have been made so easily. Woodworking patterns can be found online at very low prices. Although free patterns should be taken with caution, internet patterns can often be of equal or greater quality than the ones sold in stores. Internet patterns can be more specific, and they are easier to use diagrams or pictures. Sites will often offer discounts for returning customers or other incentives. Each pattern should include all of the specifications and materials required to complete it.

These patterns can be difficult for novices or experienced woodworkers. An experienced woodworker will be able to refer to patterns for additional guidance, while a beginner woodworker can simply use the pattern as a guide.

In order to make the instructions more easily understood, a typical woodworking pattern will include three designs. The first diagram should clearly show the materials used. The second diagram should show how different parts fit together. The third diagram should depict the finished project as well as its functionalities.

The problem with purchasing woodworking patterns from an internet source is the difficulty of tracking down the company. It can be difficult to tell if the company you buy from is using your credit card information and if your patterns are going to be delivered.

Look for companies with a history and satisfied customers.

Websites that feature a variety products from the industry are more likely than not to be legit. Websites that offer multiple products may also have more qualified staff who can help you navigate the selections.

You should also carefully read the company's refund policy. Some companies will only allow you to exchange your product. Not all products can be returned.

It is not uncommon for companies to request that their plans are not shared with any third party. Doing so could violate their privacy policy.

You should carefully consider the following factors before you choose an online pattern.

Most importantly, consider your ability to complete the project. It is possible to fail at a complicated pattern. Or, you can choose a boring pattern. Be sure to check the materials and tools that you will need for the project.

Also, make sure that you have the tools needed and determine the cost of renting or purchasing them.

Woodworking patterns are easy to find without sacrificing excitement. But the Internet can either be a paradise for woodworkers or a nightmare. When you are ready to start your next project, it is worth learning how to evaluate the quality and merchandise of a website.

However, patterns can limit the creativity of woodworkers. These patterns can be thought of as guidelines. But don't forget to personalize them! This eBook offers many tips and suggestions to help you design your own woodworking pattern or enhance an existing one.

Bedroom Plan Tips

Your bedroom is your sanctuary, a space where you can rest and relax. The bedroom can also be an external reflection of you. As such, you must carefully consider how your bedroom will appear and function. Do you want your bedroom to be comfortable and inviting? Or will it serve a purposeful, quiet retreat from the rest.

Begin by assessing the bedroom's natural light. A large amount of natural light can be used during the day to provide an alternative to expensive artificial lighting. Your bedroom plan should include plenty of windows. Large windows with slideable doors allow for lots of natural light and ventilation.

Some people have trouble sleeping due to bright light. You should include rails for thick and dark curtains to allow natural lighting to be dimmed in your room.

Wood is often chosen as the best material for creating a peaceful atmosphere. In your bedroom plan, consider including wooden floorsboards and walls.

Wooden floors, unlike ceramic tiles or marble, will retain heat. It is difficult to imagine what it would be like to walk on a cold and slippery floor every morning. Consider purchasing a soft, thick rug for the area where granite, marble, or ceramic flooring will be installed.

Artificial lighting is the best option to enhance wooden floorboards. Pin lights and shades for lamps are great options. This will create a relaxing, romantic atmosphere at nights. You should be careful not to rely on these soft lighting sources for very strong lighting. A central light source will likely still be needed.

You can add a wooden cupboard or storage space to your bedroom if it is full of clutter. A second set will keep your bedroom organized and clean.

A uniform appearance makes it easier to see. Consider buying the same color, fabric, and design for the curtains as the bed clothes. Do your best to match the color, type, and grain of wooden furniture, walling, and floorboards. This will make the room appear professional.

Mirrors can make small rooms seem larger. Mirrors can create the illusion that the space is larger than it really is.

Take into account the many factors that will impact the appearance of your bedroom when designing it. These tips will ensure your bedroom is your private sanctuary.

Deck Plan Tips

The deck of your house can make a lasting impression, or create a multitude of complaints for you. Your deck should make a strong statement for your house, as well as offer comfort and enjoyment. It is important to design a thoughtful deck plan for your home.

A good deck plan will allow you to predetermine deck use and arrange all necessary components.

The first thing you need to decide is whether your deck will connect to the house. It is also important to decide whether you will be adding railings, a ceiling, and sitting areas to your deck.

Now that you have decided on the basic structure for the deck, it is time to consider the construction materials. The quality and types of the building materials determine the cost of construction, how much maintenance it requires, and how long it will last.

Decks are outdoor structures exposed to elements and the natural climate. The building materials used should be of the highest quality.

Today decks can be made from many different materials. Wood is the most common. Wood is durable, versatile and easy to work.

The deck's frame should be made from heavy, wooden beams. For a more warm or attractive look, you can use wooden boards as the flooring.

Don't limit yourself to just building a deck from wood. Concrete and other materials are also available at your local hardware shops. They are as strong as wood. Concrete, in particular, can be used as the foundations and pad for the stairs.

Only after the deck floor has been completed should additional comforts be included, such as lighting and posts, beams or railings.

Before construction can begin, deck plans must be reviewed and approved by the building authorities in your area. The plans must be complete, and include information about the building materials and sizes. This can be difficult work for beginner woodworkers and requires specialized knowledge. Therefore, it is best to hire a licensed contractor.

The goal of your deck should be to make it a relaxing, sturdy place that you can enjoy both indoors and out.

The Kitchen Project

No matter if you are renovating an older house or building a new one, the kitchen needs to be given a lot of attention.

The kitchen is the busiest area of the house. People are always coming and going from one place to another, whether they're cooking or cleaning or just chatting. The kitchen is a hub for perishable foods and potentially hazardous electronic equipment. Family time and celebrations revolve around food, so it is important that the kitchen encourages the pursuit and enjoyment of the culinary arts.

When designing a kitchen, it's essential to think about every detail. The kitchen must be functional and easy to use. The layout of the furniture, equipment, and overall arrangement should be relaxed and uncluttered.

Find inspiration in magazines and articles on the internet. These sources offer many options and can be a great place to start planning the project. When brainstorming ideas, don't limit yourself to just home remodeling articles. Family and food magazines can be equally helpful.

Another way to be restricted is to look only at photos of completed kitchens. Look at the small details, like countertop design or cabinet placement. This will allow you to not feel obligated copying a kitchen that you like. Instead, you will create a range of appealing elements that will turn your kitchen completely personal.

Many people find it useful to create a scrapbook that contains ideas for their kitchen. Make copies of the images and other details that you like, or print them. You will have more options when you save many styles and features. This will help you to design your own kitchen.

Local home improvement stores can help you with advice and supplies. Lowe's and Home Depot offer both traditional and contemporary kitchen designs. In addition, they stock a wide range of accessories and cabinets to match.

Invite an interior decorator to visit your home. A professional opinion can give you practical ideas based upon the layout and style your kitchen. While hiring an interior designer may be costly, having someone to share ideas with is always worth it.

A kitchen remodel can be expensive and difficult. This is a decision that will be cherished for many decades. This is why you should spend a lot of time researching and exploring all possible options. These tips will help you to create a plan that you're happy with.

Bird House Plans

Growing interest in gardening and bird watching has led to a renewed interest in the outdoors. The loss of birds' natural habitats, such as trees and marshes, has prompted a greater awareness and increased involvement of people in protecting avian species.

You can attract and protect birds by building a birdhouse in your backyard. This will help to encourage them to return to the wild.

It is important to remember that building a birdhouse should not be done lightly. A bird house that is both safe and comfortable will be a good choice.

Before you begin, be familiar with the living needs of the birds in your area. Take into account the entrance's natural dimension and the size of any cavities the birds may occupy in nature.

When building the birdhouse, the first thing you should do is determine the dimensions. Once you have established the dimensions of your bird house, you can begin to consider other requirements. The bird house must be protected from direct sun and rain. Wood is the easiest material for building, but you must either paint it with a waterproof coating, or purchase waterproof-treated wood.

Be sure to countersink all bird house entrances. You can do this by making sure that the roof edges are not too close to the walls of your house. This will keep rain out of the house.

Make sure that the entrances are accessible by the bird before you start cutting them. Avoid putting pegs, or any other perches close to the entrance. These are counter-intuitive and can discourage or even stop birds from entering or exiting your house.

Ventilation is important for birds houses. There are small vents at each wall, as well as a row of holes under the roof. A drainage hole should be drilled into the floor to drain water from these small outlets.

Bright colors tend to attract birds better. Your bird house should be painted white or lighter grays. It is also possible to use neutral shades such as gray or green.

It is important to position your bird house in a way that makes it easy to clean. A ladder may be required to clean your birdhouse if it is located on stilts.

Bad planning could stop birds from using your house. So plan carefully. You can encourage birds to use your birdhouse for many years.

Chapter 12: Picking Wood

Fifften, the final product's quality will depend on how good the wood was. The key to choosing a high-quality wood is knowing how to do it correctly and the correct techniques. Here are some tips and tricks to help you choose the right wood.

What types of wood are you able to choose from?

Large areas of forest land are available in this country, where there is a large variety of wood. Woodworkers prefer a handful of types over all others because they are both high quality and attractive. You can choose from either hardwoods or softwoods. Each wood type has specific features that make it desirable for different types of projects.

Softwoods

1. Cedar

There are many varieties of cedar in the United States, but the most common one used for woodwork is the western red. The wood of the western Red is reddish in color, just like its name. Many people love its straight grain and slight aroma. The western red cedar is a softwood and ranks at 1 to 4 on the wood toughness scale. This wood is ideal for outdoor applications such as garden furniture and decks.

2. Pine

The most commonly found softwood tree species in America is the pine tree. There are several varieties including the Ponderosa (sugar, white, yellow), and the Ponderosa. Pine is easy-to-work with due to its softness and light weight. This makes pine a popular choice for indoor furniture as well as carving. The pine's color ranges from pale yellow to light-colored brown.

3. Fir

A piece of Douglas fir wood

One of the most notable features of the Fir is its grain. It is pronounced and straight with a reddish tone. The grain is not as appealing to the eye as other wood grains. This is why many woodworkers prefer to use it when they are planning to paint. One of the most valuable features of the Douglas fir is its strength, hardness and durability. This is why the Douglas fir is used so heavily in construction. Woodworkers love it because it is affordable.

4. Redwood

Redwood timber

Redwood is often used in outdoor projects because of its high water resistance. It is very similar to cedar. It is also relatively easy to use, as is the case with softwoods. Redwood's beautiful reddish color is what makes it a popular choice for decorative purposes. It is inexpensive and can be easily purchased at any local store.

Hardwoods

1. Ash

Slice of European ash

Ash is one of the most commonly used hardwoods. It has a hardness level of 4. This combined with its strength makes ash a good choice for making high strength sporting equipment like hockey sticks and bats. Ash has become more difficult to get these days. They can only been purchased through large lumber yards.

2. Birch

Silver birchwood

Birch is an affordable, easy-to-find and inexpensive option. It is very strong with a hardness around 4. Woodworkers often choose between two varieties: yellow birch and white birch. Yellow birch displays a pale yellow hue with a slight reddish tint in the hardwood. White birch however looks very similar to maple.

3. Cherry

Cherry wood

Cherry is a well-known staining wood that is easy to work with. This also enhances the natural beauty of cherry's reddishbrown heartwood. It's also extremely soft, having a hardness of 2 and making it easy to use, making it ideal when building furniture. Because it is in high demand, however, it can be harder to obtain than other woods. This makes it more expensive.

4. Mahogany

Mahogany is the most famous furniture wood. It is highly preferred for its hardness of rating 2, as well its natural beauty due its deep red hue, medium texture, straight grain, and beautiful color. It can also be stained easily, which mahogany is capable of taking in. In addition to being used for furniture, mahogany also finds a place in boatbuilding and the crafting of decorative items.

5. Maple

Maple-made bench

Hard maple and soft maple are the most common types used in woodworking. Despite the names, both maple types are hardier than other woods. Hard maple tops the scale at 5 on its hardness scale, making them difficult to work. However, soft maple is more manageable. However, they are both more stable than most woods and therefore suitable for outdoor uses. They are also fairly inexpensive when compared to other woods.

5. Oak

White oak tree

Oak is another popular wood for furniture-making. It can be found in both red and white varieties. White oak is more popular for its beauty as well as its resistance of moisture. It's ideal for outdoor pieces, such as parts for boats. Both are well-known for being strong and durable (with a hardness level of 4).

6. Poplar

Furniture made from poplar

Poplar is one of the easiest woods to work with and also has a hardness rating of only 1. Poplar isn't used as much in fine furniture, as it is less common than wood varieties with more beautiful grain. Also, poplar is almost always painted over when it is. It is still used for making cabinet drawers because of its strength, durability and cost.

7. Teak

Closeup of the teak table

Teak is known for its excellent weather resistance. It makes a great choice to make outdoor furniture and other products. Another attractive feature is its golden-brown colour. Because teak is highly sought after, it has become more difficult to obtain. It can cost as much as $24 per ft. It's also moderately difficult, coming in at 3 on the scale.

8. Walnut

Walnut has many uses beyond furniture. Because of its medium hardness (4 on the scale), and relative ease of use, it can also be used to carve and make gunstocks. You can use the intricate grain to make decorative inlays. The boards run about $8 per foot.

Selecting the right wood

Now that you know what types of wood are available, it's time for you to figure out how to choose the right one at the lumberyard for you project. Here are some points to consider.

1. Type of project

As mentioned above, different wood types are better suited for different types projects. For example, if you plan to build a simple and unadorned sidetable, you can use most of the cheaper woods. However, if it is more elaborate, a high-quality wood will show off the design's beauty more. This is not difficult for beginners because most projects give exact specifications.

2. Types

There are often many wood types that can be used to make a project. This could confuse someone who is just starting out. Knowing which wood type is more popular in your local area will help you find them easier. There are instances when softwoods may be substituted for hardwoods. They have the same strengths. The specifications will help the beginner determine the most suitable wood type.

3. Wood Grade

Once you've determined the type of wood, you can now assess its wood quality. This is especially important for pieces where wood quality is the main attraction. Wood is commonly graded according to the following: No. 3B Common, No. 3A Common, Sound Wormy, No. 2B Common, No. 2A Common, No. 2A Common and No. Wood grade is typically determined by the characteristics of the sample in lumberyards and home centers.

4. Wood Condition

Some wood planks may appear beautiful from afar. However, once you start working with them, you will notice many flaws. It is possible to not immediately see the straightness or shape of a wood board. You should inspect all pieces of wood that you purchase to make sure they are free from any defects. There are some situations where you can get around these defects. If the piece is to be cut, for example, you can simply trim the affected area.

5. Wood Condition

It can be confusing for those who are not experienced in estimating wood costs. This is easily fixed by understanding that hardwoods are more expensive than softwoods. You should also be aware that luxury woods are more difficult to get and therefore are more expensive. It is possible to save on costs by assessing which parts of the project will require such high-end wood and which parts could be done with a more affordable alternative. It is also important to consider the type and finish of the finished project. For a better price comparison, get quotations from several sellers. The following are some of these common defects that you should look for when inspecting wooden items:

1. Bow

A bow refers to the movement of the wood from end to end.

2. Cup

A cup has the wood bent across one of its faces.

3. Crook

When the wood is warped along its perimeter, it becomes a crook.

4. Twist

A twist is the severe bending or warping of wood.

5. Wood Knot

An imperfection is when the grain pieces around a discolored, circular area. A knothole can be described as a hole where the grain parts again.

6. Split

A split can be described as a crack in wood.

7. Take a look

A check is defined as a crack along the annular growth bands of the wood but not the entire thickness.

8. Wane

Waning can occur when there are still bits of bark or wood along the board's edges.

Chapter 13: Woodworking Tools

When you have decided to take up woodworking as a career, it is important that you get all the tools necessary. Most likely, most of the basic tools are already available in your home. You might still want to purchase additional pieces of equipment. To make sure you are always prepared for any unexpected situations, it might be worth replacing some of your tools. In any event, you need to know the basics of hand and power tools. Each category will be covered, along with the essential tools needed. We will also examine miscellaneous tools that can be included in your shop tool kit.

Hand Tools

A range of woodworking tools

Because they are usually easy to obtain and affordable, hand tools make it the easiest way to start woodworking. Below are some essential hand tools that every basic woodworking tool kit should include.

1. Hammer

The clawhammer is one of the most easily recognized tools for woodwork. You can not only use it to drive nails into wood but you can also remove them with the clawed tip. The clawed ends also serve as counterweights to balance the hammerhead. It can be useful for many other tasks.

The weight of the hammer is an important factor to consider when purchasing one. A heavier head means more power for every stroke. This makes driving nails easier. This might make it a bit harder to control. When buying a new hammer, another consideration is the handle size. The longer the handle, you can swing the hammer faster and increase force. The preferred weight for a claw-hammer is approximately 450 grams.

2. Hand Saw

Another tool used in woodworking is the handsaw. Even with power tools like the circular saw or the jigsaw being available, woodworkers who are experienced consider at least two different handsaws essential.

Ripsaw

Crosscut saw

There are many hand saws available, but the two most essential types to have in your starting kit are the ripsaw (or crosscut) and the crosscut. They cut wood in two different ways. The crosscut saw cuts across the grain and the ripsaw cuts along the grain. The number of teeth, also known as teeth per indent/TPI, determines which saw should cut a particular wood stock. Higher TPI saws are better for smaller stock. A lower TPI saw is more useful for cutting larger stocks.

You can purchase a saw with interchangeable knives if you don't need to handle two separate tools.

3. Tape Measure

A measure for retractable tape

For wood projects, accuracy is key. You want every piece to fit exactly to the dimensions. A tape measure is better than using a ruler because it is compact and can be carried around easily. It is best to have a 25-foot retractable tap measure. Anything more than that will cause the retract mechanism malfunction.

The strength of the hook at your tape measure is an important aspect to consider when purchasing it. It is possible for the hook to become loose and slide out of place. This could cause a significant error in your measurements. Keep the tape from rolling back too hard to avoid damaging the tab.

4. Screwdriver

Screwdriver set includes interchangeable bits. The bits are standard sizes and are suitable for general use.

If you are looking to quickly disassemble parts of a joint, screwdrivers will be useful. But they can be quite frustrating when you don't have just the right size of screwdriver. A good screwdriver set should have the most common sizes for Phillips and flat-head screws. It is also helpful to have Torx drivers and star drivers, even though these are rarer.

5. Chisel

The chisel, which is commonly associated with woodcarving, is perhaps one of the lesser-known of the basic hand tools. The chisel, however, can be used for many purposes. It can be used to clean up joints and make saw cuts. The chisel can also be used to pry apart two parts that have been joined.

A selection of woodworking chisels

It's a smart idea to buy multiple sizes when purchasing chisels. You will have a longer life span if you choose chisels that are made of high-carbon alloy steel. These can withstand hammer hits well, so make sure to get hardwood grips with metal caps.

6. Hand Plane

Block Plane

Even though the handplane is often overlooked by woodworkers beginning to learn, it is an important tool in any woodworking kit. It can be used to shape and trim wood according to measurements. For novices, a basic block plane is an excellent choice. You'll be surprised to learn that older block planes are a good choice, because the quality of steel used for parts is often better.

Power Tools

These power tools make it easier to complete common woodworking tasks faster and more efficiently. There are two kinds of corded power tools. These tools need to be plugged into a wall outlet. Cordless tools have their own battery packs. Most power tools come with a range attachments that can be used to accomplish the work of multiple tools.

1. Circular Saw

Although the circular see is often considered more of an instrument for carpentry work, it has become essential for woodworkers. The circular saw is able to do saw-able cuts. It can also be adjusted to make precise cuts by using clamps. This is great for working with plywood or fiberboard.

Similar to the hand-saw, the number and type of teeth are important for a circular or saw blade. A blade with more teeth makes it easier to make precise slices.

2. Jig saw

It can be difficult to cut curves out of wood with regular saws. A jigsaw can make the job easier as it gives you more control over how the cut is made. Orbital action would be a great feature to have with a new jigsaw. Orbital action is a jigsaw that angles the blade forward to make a smoother cut. This is in contrast to standard jigsaws, which only move the blade down and up. You will find this feature in more expensive units.

3. Table Saw

For many, the tablesaw would be their first major purchase. This is because it is where most of the work will take place. A table saw allows you to easily cut large pieces of lumber as well as smaller pieces. Many table saws have components that can be used to cut wood at different thicknesses and angles.

4. Drill for Power

Another common task is drilling holes. This is where you'll be surprised to discover that a corded power tool drill will work better than a handheld one. The reason is that corded power drills tend to be less expensive and provide more power over time.

5. Router

The router is a useful tool that beginners will appreciate for a wide range of tasks. A stationary model is good for beginners as it can be used to complete most tasks. You should choose a unit with at minimum 2 HP, so it can handle larger bits.

6. Random Orbital Sander

Random Orbital Sander w/ Sanding Disks

Sanding is a difficult woodworking task. You'll likely spend hours trying achieve the perfect smoothness. The random orbital-sander makes it easier and takes away the hassle of rubbing sandpaper on the wood. Another advantage of the random orbital-sander is its ability to reduce the appearance of visible sanding marks. The random motion of the sander makes it easier to see the wood's grain and pattern.

Miscellaneous Tools & Items

There are other tools you need to have in your shop's inventory. These items can be useful in a range of tasks. They also come in handy when you are looking for improvised tools.

1. Clamps

Clamps can be considered one of the most important tools in your shop. You can use them to secure the wood beam to be bent. There are many types available in clamps:

corner clamps with C clamps, bar clamps for spring clamps or face clamps.

2. Pliers

Although pliers are most commonly used for electronic and electrical work, there are tons of other uses. As with clamps, pliers can also be used for holding pieces of wood during work. Pliers can also serve as a temporary wrench to loosen bolts from wooden panels or as a lever for prying pieces of wood.

3. Niveaux

When building items such as cabinets or tables, it is essential that they are level with the ground. You can check this by using a level. A basic level consists of a small clear cylindrical with a liquid inside and a bubble within.

4. Speed Square & Builder's Square

A speedsquare is a tool that allows the woodworker or machinist to see if pieces must be in right angles. The speedsquare is basically an L-shaped ruler.

5. Marking tools

The carpenter's and chalk are the two most used tools for marking. You should always have them on hand. The chalk is the everyday type that you can buy at school supplies shops.

6. Work Is Important

Particularly useful for those who must deal with tight spaces, work stands are a great option. These are useful for holding tools so they aren't lying around. A work stand can be very useful if you have to transfer between rooms.

7. Air Compressor

Most power tools are electrically powered. But, some power tools, such as nail guns, can be powered with compressed air. The versatility of air compressors is not limited to powering pneumatic tools. They can also be used for running other equipment.

Chapter 14: Crosscutting Jig

Easy to make, the shop-built tool will ensure your crosscuts meet the stock edges. Select 1/2 inch plywood for edge guide and 3/4 inches plywood for fence.

The dimensions of your jig depend upon the width and thickness of the stock you are cutting as well the width and thickness of your base plate.

When you are cutting, ensure that the edge guide is at the same length as your work piece. It should also be wide enough to clamp to it without getting in the way.

The fence should not be wider than 4 inches and longer than both the edge guide or base plate. The two pieces of the Jig should be screwed together. A try square will check to make sure that they are in perfect vertical alignment.

The jig can be used by simply clamping it to the piece of work as you would for standard crosscuts. Be sure the blade is aligned with the marking on your work piece.

Keep the fence parallel to the edge of your work piece. To make the cut, you can run the saw along an edge guide.

The first use will trim the fence at the edge of the blade with the jig. You can make further cuts by clamping the jig on the work piece and aligning the fence with your stock's cutting mark.

How to cut thick stock

Crosscutting stock more dense than the maximum saw blade depth allows you to make intersecting cuts. First mark a cut line on one of the stock's faces. Then use a trysquare to extend that line around the three other faces.

Then clamp the workpiece to the sawhorses. Align the blade and the cutting line. Then, put an edge guide against a saw's baseplate and clamp it to work piece.

Adjust the depth of the cut to a minimum of one-half the thickness. Then, make the cut. Flip the workpiece upside down and place the clamps, the edge guide, and complete the cutting.

How to cut large panels

To stop a panel from sagging during a cut, and to prevent the blade from binding, support it on a platform made of sawhorses 2x4. Two boards should measure approximately 3 inches each on either side.

Position the panel onto the 2-by-4s. Then, clamp it in place. You can clamp a straightedge guide to your panel for greater accuracy. Aligning your blade with the cutting edge, cut slowly and steadily using both of your hands to guide the saw. Keep the blade from bending by inserting kerfspliters along the way

Crosscutting:

You will need enough 2-by-4s to support your panel at 12-inch intervals. Set the stock on the boards by shifting two of them so that they rest at least 3 inches to either side.

To cut, lower to one knee. With both hands, grip the saw. Use your balance to cut steady and steadily. To minimize your weight, place the 2-by-4 to the side of cutting line.

The shop-built straightedge tool makes it simple to rip plywood panels. The base should be made from 1/4-inch plywood. For the edge, you can use 3/4-inch plywood.

Glue one end of the strip parallel to that of the base. Cut the base to the correct width for the saw.

To use the Jig, mark a cutting line on the panel and then clamp the stock to the platform of 2-by-4s. These will be stable over the sawhorses. The guide should be clamped to the panel.

Do the same as a regular rip cut. Keep the saw's bottom plate in line with the edge strip.

How to Use a Guide for Cutting Miters

After clamping the work piece to sawhorses you can set a protractor/miter guide at the angle you desire to cut. Align the sawblade with the cutting line of the work piece.

Place the protractor on top of the stock. Hold its guiding edge against its base plate and its fence against its edge. While you're cutting, hold the guide and saw in your hands.

How to Make a Belvedere Cut?

Set the desired angle by loosening the bevel adjustment knob. Secure the workpiece to the sawhorses.

After aligning the blade with your cutting mark, you can then butt the edge guide against the base plate of the saw. Secure the guide to your board. Then, clamp the guide to the board.

How to Cut a Taper

Place the stock on the work surface. The cutting line should extend several inches beyond its edge. You will need to position the workpiece so that the cutting line is at the edge of the board.

After aligning the blade with the cutting mark place an edgeguide on top of the stock. If necessary, measure the distance between the guide and the base plate to ensure the guide is parallel.

Cut the material as you would a standard-sized rip. As the waste Step becomes narrower, hold onto the saw.

Guide to Meter & Crosscutting

You can use the jig to create multipurpose edges guides that are useful for making 45-degree miter cuts and crosscuts. It can be made of 3/4-inch plywood.

Cut a triangle using one 90-degree angle (or two 45 degrees) and two 45 degree angles (or any other variation that has a 3-4-5 ratio).

Screw the fences onto the base. One on each side. The other is at 45 degrees. The fences need to be flush with jig base edges. The jig can be used to cut miter pieces by clamping the workpiece on the sawhorses.

Then align your saw's blade to the stock. Next, place the long side of your jig against a saw's base plate. The guide's fence must be flush against the work piece.

Secure the jig and make the cut just like you would with a standard saw. The saw should remain in the same position as the jig during the entire operation. You can crosscut by using the other side.

Advanced cuts

The versatility of a circle saw can be greatly enhanced by a little imagination and the use of the correct jigs. This tool cannot replace a tablesaw and radial arms saw, but it can dimension stock.

It is sometimes difficult to use a bigger stationary saw. You can instead use your portable tool to cut joints for cabinetmaking ventures.

To achieve precise results with dadoes, miters, and rabbits, use a fine-tooth shaver when you are performing these tasks.

Although the circular saw does not cut wood as quickly as the tablesaw or radial-arm saw, it is portable and can be used in places that aren't accessible to stationary machines.

A saw can cut through a panel's middle, making a rectangle, or cutting around the edges. You can also make arcs or circles with a series of straight cuts.

1 – Cutting kerfs inside the dado outline

Mark the width on the stock's front face with a pencil, and clamp it to a surface.

* Place a mark on the work piece's edge as a reference point. Set the cutting depth of blade according to the dado.

* Place a clamp on an edge guide to prevent the saw's cutting beyond one of the width markings.

* Repeat the procedure for the reverse side of the dambo.

* Grab the saw with both hands and use one guide to ride the base plate.

* Now run the saw along a second support to cut the other end of the channel.

* To eliminate as many waste as possible, saw a variety of kerfs between both cuts, working at about 1/8-inch intervals.

2 - Chiseling the waste

* Holding the wood chisel at a slight angle strike the handle of the mallet with a wooden mallet.

* Always ensure that the beveled face of the chisel points up.

* When the bulk waste has been removed, trim the dado to make it smooth and even.

How do you make a plunge cut?

1 – Biting into the stock

1. Attach the workpiece to the sawhorses. 2. Align the blade on one of your cutting lines.

* Now clamp an edge guide on the work piece so that it is flush against your saw's base plate.

* Make your guide longer than the marking mark, and high enough so that it can guide the saw when the saw is tilted up.

* With one hand, pull the lower guard of the blade back and the other grip the handle tightly. Next, place the toe end of the base plate on a work piece and tilt the saw forward in order to raise the blade clear of the stock.

* Hold the back edge of the blade at the top of the cutting lines.

* Make sure the saw is flatten on the workpiece. Lift the blade guard off the workpiece and move the tool forward.

* When the blade has reached the end of its cutting line, switch off the saw.

* Make plunge cuts along three of the remaining cutting lines.

2 – Completing the plunge cut

* The circular blade of a portable powersaw will cause a little waste at the end and beginning of each cut.

* Square corners with a sabersaw (or a handsaw), making sure to keep your blade vertical when you cut.

Chapter 15: Woodworking Plans-What To Expect In Woodworking Plans

A woodworking hobby is something that everyone enjoys. Woodwork is great for those who enjoy using their hands. Woodworking is a job that requires attention to detail and measurement. Quality woodworking plans will be useful as measurements and information are vital to the success or a project.

While woodwork patterns can be found in most cases, they are not all the same quality. It's not as important to select the right one as its size. The most important thing is the level of expertise. Plan should be adapted to hobbyists' level of skill.

Woodworking plans are only as good as the knowledge and understanding you have. It is important to have a list of all supplies required for the project. It allows you to plan ahead so you don't have to stop working for something you didn't expect. You will not have any leftover tools if you are using effective woodworking techniques. You'll spend more on a job if your resources are wasted.

The best woodworking techniques can help you save time and money. This will ensure that you don't get distracted or make costly mistakes. Although woodworking projects are not always easy, it shouldn't be difficult. Projects that have very complicated ideas can often cost more than expected.

There will be a lengthy list of necessary materials in some project plans. Because of vague directions, it is not recommended to increase the content. It will ruin a fun project if you use low-quality plans for woodworking. You might find it frustrating to have to purchase extra materials for mistakes that were not made.

Woodworking techniques are more efficient and less costly than traditional methods. However, good woodworking plans can have certain distinguishing features. A good plan will outline the materials and equipment necessary to complete the project. Without a clear plan, you'll never have the right equipment or tools. When that happens, you will realize you have made a greater investment than you thought.

Although it is important that you have a list of all materials, the recommendations will be essential. The steps will be clearly explained in the recommendations. Preparations should be carefully planned and all necessary details established. Plans that include illustrations or pictures are more effective than plans without them. You should include a photograph of the final product when designing woodworking projects. This will allow you to get a clear idea of the vision.

Along with maps or pictures, a list detailing the measurements for each step should be included. A detailed list with measurements ensures that each cut is correct. This is essential because any measurement that is incorrect would result in the demise of the entire project. Before you begin, make sure to carefully review the instructions.

Woodworking plans play an important role in any woodworking endeavor. Many plans can be a hindrance to success or failure. Before any hobbyist begins a project, he/she must read the plans carefully.

You can find the best woodwork rankings at tedswoodworkratings.com.

Are you looking for a new hobby or skill? You can get woodwork plans to help you learn the craft.

Many woodworking schedules work as an action guide for every job. You will keep each project going with a set woodworking plans. If you have any other ideas, you will plan what to do and how.

Good woodworking plans provide a detailed list of materials and all necessary instruments for making a wooden object. Also, step by step instructions. What color would your house look like if you were to paint it? How much paint would you need? What tools do you need such as paint brushes, cups, scrappers and other tools? The tools that you will need.

To plan your workshop you will need to know what kind and how to mount the shelving. A plan would include a list containing all the materials required and all the tools needed to finish a woodworking task. It would also work for any other type or idea.

A collection of tools, such as wrenches or screwdrivers, is required for lawn furniture. If you need to take care of your lawn, equipment such as a mower, weed-eater, and maybe some hedge clippers are required.

The woodwork plans will provide you with step-by-step instructions on how to cut and arrange your wood. For bringing together other things, the same guidance is available. While you may have to cut content to fit the space, the assembly process works in the correct order.

After you have made an airplane or a car, you can finish it by applying decals or paint. When you create something out of wooden, you would then stain or paint. You can draw parallels between woodworking as well as many other crafts.

It is easy to see that woodworking can be compared to other crafts like sewing, scrapbooking or cutting. Your imagination and creativity are your tools to mix and match elements such as paint and dye.

You visit the closest home improvement store to get the required equipment and supplies. You follow the instructions provided in your plans. For many years, you'll love your high-quality furniture.

If you want to be successful, start with something simple. It gives you confidence to take on bigger and better projects if you are successful in your first job. The basics of woodwork will be taught to you by even the simplest jobs.

It is easier than ever to get into woodworking, and you can do quality work with the modern tools. You can get high-quality furniture made of real wood, which is durable and affordable without having to buy a complete kit.

Not only can you learn about different wood types but also the complexity of veneers and exotic hardwoods. It is easy to see the limitless possibilities in woodworking. Woodwork can be a great way to save money on home projects. What you once hired, you can now do yourself. Your house will become the hub of all your ideas, and add an individual touch to your home. You will be grateful when someone adds value to a piece that you made. It is incredibly rewarding and makes it even more fun.

Woodworking is not cheap, but it's also one of my favorite hobbies. It's amazing to make something out of nothing but raw wood. You don't matter how proficient you are in woodworking. There is always more to learn. Woodwork is an endless hobby.

Who are Woodworkers and What Are Their Skills?

There used to exist two woodworkers' myths: one, there was the cranky teacher in the shop who gave children who didn't like it a boring class and another, the Grandpa, who worked hard in his garage to make a rare birdhouse.

These stereotypes don't hold anymore. Online forums and the abundance in tools and materials make woodworking easier than ever.

In the last ten year, there have been two types of woodworkers.

First: Women were woodworkers not so long ago. Woodworkers have become commonplace among women. Woodworking is a skill that can be learned by all.

Second was the population explosion in millennia. This included people in their twenties, thirties and forefathers. People who work in Silicon Valley are constantly looking for something to do with their faces, and have some kind of office job.

What is the difference in production and woodworking?

Producers are a relatively new concept. It was developed in the last decade. This is an umbrella term that refers to people who love working in various craft fields. This could include woodworking as well as metalworking, epoxying and concreting. We are all producers.

Woodworkers are producers that are primarily interested in the craft and practice of wood-building. Our projects may include other materials but the main focus is always wood. It's an inexpensive, timeless material you can use to create beautiful things.

What's the difference between Woodworking, Carpentry and Woodworking?

This may sound a little vague, but I tend not to think of carpenters only as architects, builders, or even houses. Build a building.

Framing a home isn't as simple as building it from beams, posters and 2x4s. Woodworking is often used for furniture construction and the creation of other moving objects. It doesn't matter if woodworkers are also called carpenters.

Woodworking Plans, Projects

Many people have been woodworking for years and have produced excellent plans. Woodworking plans are available for novices and experts alike. Woodworking is without a doubt one of the most effective ways to create something. Woodwork allows you to enjoy your weekend more constructively. It's a fun experience to create something wonderful.

It's eye-catching to see furniture displayed in shops and showrooms. They are however expensive. This has led many people to choose wood as an option to expensive materials. The simple act of turning raw materials like MDF sheets or pine boards into furniture can help you save substantial money. When renovating your house, you can save a lot of money by buying new chairs, desks and tables as well as cabinets.

Sometimes furniture prices are so high that homeowners might not consider buying it. You can still make wonderful furniture for your home. Many wood species are affordable before becoming furniture. Their costs are skyrocketing. This is due in part to high transport and design and crafts costs as well as labor costs that are out of reach. Homeowners will find it easier to convert raw woods and artwork into their preferred furnishings. These plans include woodworking.

Chapter 16: Preparing A Surface

Preparing the surface is essential before you can begin on your dream project. After you are done, staining and applying a topcoat won't cover up a surface that isn't adequately prepared. Preparing the surface allows for easier staining and painting. Preparing the wood surface will ensure that no splinters can cause your project to be sore. This will make your wood ready for use.

1. Check out the Wood

You should inspect the wood you've purchased before you buy it. Note any cracks, holes or splits. This should not be done after the project is completed. Instead, prepare the wood first.

2. Fill Holes and Cracks

Wood filler and/or glue can be used to fill holes in wood that are split, cracked or damaged. Don't be lazy and just fill the hole with wood glue. It will require more sanding to complete the job. Sanding too often can result in a decrease in the wood's thickness and a poor project outcome. Instead, use the screwdriver's point to place the filler in the hole. Allow the filler to dry before you place it in the hole. This should allow you to sand the filler again with paper.

3. It is possible to sand it!

Sanding is vital, even if you feel your project doesn't require it. It can be used to remove any small scratches or nicks you may see when you apply stain. Sanding helps to remove any glaze left behind by factory's plane blades. Neglecting to sand your wood can cause glaze to form and block the wood's pores from setting the stain or finishing coat.

4. Do a test first

While I understand that you're eager to get started with your woodworking projects, you should first make sure to test your stain and technique on some scrap material. You didn't skip this step and you don't need to waste precious wood!

5. Use the Wood Conditioner

Conditioner should be used regularly. Do not skip this step or your stain may blotch. Staining wood without properly preparing it is a sure way to ruin a product.

Sanding

All sandpapers are different. Woodworking is not the same as sandpaper. There are specific uses for each type of sandpaper. As a guide, consider the following:

Coarse Sandpaper

This grit is below #100. It's used to quickly remove wood or old coatings. This is used when a floor needs to be refinished or windows and doors need to be rehung.

Medium Sandpaper

This grit will suit your wood preparation needs. It can be used to remove small scratches, marks, and edges from cutting that could lead to splinters. The most common sandpaper used to prepare sanding most wood products is coarse or medium.

Fine Sandpaper

(#220-grit). After the project has been assembled, this grit is recommended for a second polish. The wood can be stained or coated with clear protective finish after the second sanding.

The Right Sander

A lot of woodworking projects are not difficult enough to be done without an electric sander. To work with small, detailed projects in wood, you only need to cut or tear a piece of the grit sheet into fourths. Each piece should fit comfortably under your three fingers.

For flat, large surfaces, you will need an orbital sander or an electric palm. But, you can do just fine without one. Wrapping the sandpaper around a piece of wood or scrap wood can help if the surface becomes too large. Now you can sand more easily with this leverage.

If you work with hardwood flooring, beltsanders won't be needed. They can create more scratches than the sanders can remove and also take out more wood than you need.

Be on the lookout for Saw Dust!

Don't rush so that you can immediately apply a finish or coat after the second sanding. Dust can ruin your smooth finish. To achieve professional results, make sure that you have removed any dust that could affect your final coat.

Conclusion

It was a pleasure to share this information with you. Woodworking can be very rewarding and may even make your life better. Making woodwork can open up new possibilities and help you to build your skills. Woodworking can be as timeless as our lives. It's a rare skill that has been around since its inception. Next, you need to choose a career field. Think about the time it will take to complete each project, how much you are willing to invest, and what work space you have. This will help narrow down your options and allow you to choose a specific area. With repetition, you will build your skills. Don't expect to create a perfectly crafted and beautiful table the first time. Have fun with your work and explore new methods. Learn a new skill or two and you will be a master at woodworking! Get started with woodworking. You'll be glad you learned this skill.

www.ingramcontent.com/pod-product-compliance
Lightning Source LLC
Chambersburg PA
CBHW050411120526
44590CB00015B/1925